Essentials) of
PSYCHOLOGICAL ASSESSMENT
Series

Everything you need to know to administer, interpret, and score the major psychological tests... the quick-reference guides written by the experts.

Each book features:
Bulleted lists • Call-out boxes • Sample reports • Completely cross-referenced material • Quick-reference graphics with standardization data

I'd like to order the following ESSENTIALS of Psychological Assessment:

❑ WAIS-III Assessment / 28295-2 / $29.95

❑ CAS Assessment / 29015-7 / $29.95

❑ Millon Inventories Assessment / 29798-4 / $29.95

❑ Forensic Psychological Assessment / 33186-4 / $29.95

❑ Bayley Scales of Infant Dev II Assessment / 32651-8 / $29.95

❑ Myers-Briggs Type Indicator® Assessment / 33239-9 / $29.95

Please send this order form with your payment (credit card or check) to:
John Wiley & Sons Publishing, Attn: M. Fellin
605 Third Avenue, New York, NY 10158

Name _____

Affiliation _____

Address _____

City/State/Zip _____

Phone _____ E-mail _____

Credit Card: ❑ Mastercard ❑ Visa ❑ American Express
(All orders subject to credit approval)

Card Number_____

Exp Date _____

Signature_____

TO ORDER BY PHONE, CALL 1-

D11153820

Essentials of Psychological Assessment Series
Series Editors, Alan S. Kaufman and Nadeen L. Kaufman

Essentials

of Bayley Scales of Infant Development– II Assessment

Maureen M. Black and
Kathleen Matula

John Wiley & Sons, Inc.
NEW YORK • CHICHESTER • WEINHEIM • BRISBANE • SINGAPORE • TORONTO

This book is printed on acid-free paper. ∞
Copyright © 2000 by John Wiley & Sons, Inc. All rights reserved.
Published simultaneously in Canada.

"Bayley Scales" are registered trademarks of The Psychological Corporation Company.

This publication is designed to provide accurate and authoritative information in regard to the subject matter covered. It is sold with the understanding that the publisher is not engaged in rendering professional services. If legal, accounting, medical, psychological or any other expert assistance is required, the services of a competent professional person should be sought.

Library of Congress Cataloging-in-Publication Data:
Black, Maureen M.
    Essentials of Bayley scales of infant development–II assessment / Maureen M. Black and Kathleen Matula.
        p.   cm. — (The essentials of psychological assessment series)
    Includes bibliographical references and index.
    ISBN 0-471-32651-8 (paper : alk. paper)
    1. Bayley Scales of Infant Development.   I. Matula, Kathleen.
II. Title.   III. Series.
    RJ51.D48B52   1999
    618.92'89075—dc21   99-34622
                                                              CIP

Printed in the United States of America.
10 9 8 7 6 5 4 3 2 1

To our children, Shaunti Black, Maresa Black, and Matthew Nicholas DiSiena, who have brought the Bayley Scales wonderfully alive and helped us treasure the complexities of infancy and childhood.

CONTENTS

SERIES PREFACE

I n the *Essentials of Psychological Assessment* series, our goal is to provide the reader with books that deliver key practical information in the most efficient and accessible style. The series features instruments in a variety of domains, such as cognition, personality, education, and neuropsychology. For the experienced clinician, books in the series will offer a concise yet thorough way to master utilization of the continuously evolving supply of new and revised instruments, as well as a convenient method for keeping up to date on the tried-and-true measures. The novice will find here a prioritized assembly of all the information and techniques that must be at one's fingertips to begin the complicated process of individual psychological diagnosis.

Wherever feasible, visual shortcuts to highlight key points are utilized alongside systematic, step-by-step guidelines. Chapters are focused and succinct. Topics are targeted for an easy understanding of the essentials of administration, scoring, interpretation, and clinical application. Theory and research are continually woven into the fabric of each book, but always to enhance clinical inference, never to sidetrack or overwhelm. We have long been advocates of "intelligent" testing—the notion that a profile of test scores is meaningless unless it is brought to life by the clinical observations and astute detective work of knowledgeable examiners. Test profiles must be used to make a difference in the child's or adult's life, or why bother to test? We want this series to help our readers become the best intelligent testers they can be.

In *Essentials of Bayley Scales of Infant Development–II Assessment* the authors describe how the revised Bayley Scales provide reliable and valid measures of infant development that can be used to describe normal development, to diagnose developmental delays or disabilities, and to plan and evaluate early intervention programs. The Bayley Scales have been instrumental in the burgeoning field of infancy, contributing to the understanding of early information processing skills, to the impact of environmental factors on development, and to the importance of early intervention for infants at risk for developmental delays. The book places the Bayley Scales within the context of ongoing clinical research issues and provides clinicians, researchers, and others with an analysis of the strengths and weaknesses of the Bayley Scales of Infant Development–II.

Alan S. Kaufman, Ph.D., and Nadeen L. Kaufman, Ed.D., Series Editors
Yale University School of Medicine

BSID-II ASSESSMENT MADE SIMPLE

The Bayley Scales of Infant Development (BSID) were published in 1969, and the revision (the second edition) was published in 1993. In addition to restandardizing the norms, the age range of the BSID-II was extended down to 1 month of age and up to 42 months, many research-based items with demonstrated predictive validity were added, and items were modernized using materials that facilitated infection control, reduced gender and racial bias, and were more attractive to young children. The BSID-II was developed with extensive field testing and feedback from clinicians and researchers, including data from children with developmental risks and delays. Despite these changes, the structure of the BSID-II remained similar to the BSID with Mental and Motor Scales and a newly developed Behavior Rating Scale to replace the Infant Behavior Record.

Over the past several decades there has been increasing concern about infant and toddler development and the impact of early intervention. With federal legislation mandating states to provide early intervention services to children under age 3 who qualify for special services, there is a need for valid and reliable methods to evaluate young children. It is not surprising that one of the primary uses of the Bayley Scales is to examine the development of infants who are suspected of having delayed or atypical development to assist in determining their eligibility for early intervention services and to track their progress.

Infant development is a burgeoning field that includes professionals in many fields, including psychology, pediatrics, neurology, education, and psychiatry. The survival rate for premature infants has increased dramatically, leaving more infants at risk for developmental delays. At the same time, researchers, clinicians, and educators have recognized the information processing capabilities of infants, have documented variations in brain development and neurochemical production, and have examined how factors at the environmental, family, and individual levels influence early development. Many professionals rely on the Bayley Scales to provide reliable and valid measures of infant development.

The intent of this book is to facilitate an understanding of the strengths and weaknesses of the BSID-II in evaluating infants. The book is written for clinicians, researchers, educators, students, and others who use the BSID-II.

Essentials

of Bayley Scales of Infant
Development–II Assessment

One

OVERVIEW

The purpose of the *Essentials of Bayley Scales of Infant Development–II Assessment* is to highlight and expand the information provided in the Bayley Scales of Infant Development–II (BSID-II) manual. This book is designed to serve as an addition to the test manual and to facilitate the administration and interpretation of the test. It provides a discussion of the foundations of infant assessment as well as the development of the Bayley Scales. Additionally, the book uses "Rapid Reference," "Caution," and "Don't Forget" boxes to make some of the information most relevant to the user more readily accessible. The *Essentials of Bayley Scales of Infant Development–II Assessment* is intended to address the needs of clinicians and researchers who are assessing the cognitive, motor, and behavioral development of infants and young children.

INFANT DEVELOPMENT

The study of infant and child development, or developmental psychology as it is known today, dates back to the naturalistic observations of Johann Heinrich Pestalozzi in the 18th century. By the late 1800s and early 1900s, a contingency of psychologists around the world (Alfred Binet in France; Wilhelm Preyer in Germany; G. Stanley Hall, James Mark Baldwin, and John B. Watson in the United States) acknowledged that development took place from conception and continued throughout life, with increasing complexity (Cairns, 1983). Some of the earliest work in developmental psychology grew from the study of biological systems, and to that end Wilhelm Preyer has been attributed with a landmark publication, *Die Seele des Kindes* (The mind of the child) in 1882. He approached the development of the human child from a background in physiology and comparative development, and proposed an

I

objective, methodological study of children through rigorous observation and an ecological approach. Preyer addressed the development of children's perceptions, motivation, and "intellect" (i.e., language and social cognition).

G. Stanley Hall is often regarded as the founder of developmental psychology. Not only was he the first president of the American Psychological Association in 1892, but he also founded the first scientific journal that addressed psychological issues as applied to children. His systematic studies of development included the entire life span, with scholarly writings about early childhood, adolescence, and old age.

By the beginning of the 20th century there was growing concern in the fields of medicine, social work, and education for the welfare of children (Cairns, 1983). As more attention was being paid to child development, funding for research grew, and in the 1920s research institutes began to spring up across the United States. The topic of study at the institutes ranged from intelligence, memory, perception, emotion, personality, and motivation to motor development (Sears, Maccoby, & Levin, 1957). These were topics of interest in the biological or medical and educational fields that were influencing the study of developmental psychology in the 19th century and early part of the 20th century. The origins of many other constructs studied in child development in the latter part of the first half of the 20th century, such as attachment, dependency, aggression, sibling relations, gender-role development, achievement motivation, and the influences of child-rearing, may be traced to psychoanalytic theory. Theorists such as Sigmund Freud, Erik Erikson, and Alfred Adler, while building their theories primarily on retrospective accounts of development, assigned significance to the roles of parents in children's development. By the 1930s and 1940s theories of child development were broadened to include social learning theory. During the latter part of the 20th century, theories of child development were broadened further to incorporate the transactional effects that children and caregivers have on one another, together with an ecological perspective that incorporates influences from the community and culture (Bronfenbrenner, 1979; Sameroff & Chandler, 1975).

In contrast, there was only fleeting interest in infant development prior to the mid-20th century, primarily because both scientists and the lay public regarded infants as helpless, dependent organisms whose perceptions were undifferentiated and whose movements were dominated by reflexes. However, as scientists learned to use systematic observation, they recognized both common patterns and individual differences in infants' abilities to process sensory information and to organize their responses. Not only could infants differentiate within sensory modalities, but they could also demonstrate choices through voluntary movements, such as suck patterns, visual gaze, or turning to sound. During the past several decades, infant research has flourished. The expansion of conceptual models to include the processing capabilities of infants, together with technological advances in brain imaging, have led to a more sophisticated understanding of the impact of early experiences on both the structure of the brain and early child development (Gunnar, 1998).

The first 3 years of life is a period of rapid brain growth that provides a "window of opportunity" for early learning. Using longitudinal data from the Berkeley Growth Study, Bayley and Schaefer (1964) reported on the mental and physical development of individuals over 36 years. There was a great deal of individual variability in scores, particularly during the first 3 years of life. However, there were complex but consistent patterns linking behavior during the first 3 years of life with cognitive performance at 18 and 36 years of age. In addition, children whose mothers were nurturant and understanding during the first 3 years had better cognitive development as adults. In more recent research, Hart and Risley (1995) demonstrated a link between early parent communication and later school performance, and they concluded that infants who are not exposed to an enriching environment may miss an important developmental opportunity. Findings such as these illustrate the importance of the early years and the critical role that the caregiving environment has on children's early development.

PURPOSE OF ASSESSING INFANT DEVELOPMENT

The origins of infant assessments are often traced to the work of Arnold Gesell, a physician and psychologist at the Yale Clinic of Child Development. Gesell had been influenced by Charles Darwin's work—not only in his comparative studies of animals but also in his interest in the growth and development of children. In the early 1920s Gesell compiled a schedule of tasks for infants ages 4, 6, 9, 12, and 18 months of age and 2, 3, 4, and 5 years of age (Gesell, 1925). By identifying predictable stages of development for the brain and visual and motor systems, Gesell hoped to document maturation and to include assessments of behavior and development into children's well-child exams so that physicians could provide families with prescriptive and predictive recommendations (Gesell, 1948).

Infant assessments such as the Gesell System of Developmental Diagnosis (Gesell, 1925) and Cattell Infant Intelligence Test (Cattell, 1940), as well as the Bayley Scales of Infant Development (Bayley, 1969), originated in the child development centers around the United States that were established in the early part of the 20th century. These early assessments were designed to catalog an infant's level of development at various ages and to establish normative data.

Toward the latter half of the 20th century and particularly in the last few decades, infant assessment has focused on the need to evaluate infants at risk for developmental delay. With recent advances in medical technology, many premature and medically challenged infants are surviving. However, rates of cerebral palsy and developmental disabilities have increased (Hack et al., 1994). Infant assessments are needed to determine whether infants are developing at an expected rate, whether they are eligible for early intervention services, and whether the early intervention is effective in improving their rate of development.

Within the last 20 years, society has also become increasingly concerned about individuals with disabilities. The concern encompasses the rights of all individuals to an equal opportunity for an education and occupation. Although school-aged children were the first group to be targeted for educational and social services, the age has been extended to birth. The Education of the Handicapped Act (EHA) was passed in 1975 and went into effect in 1977 to ensure special education and related services to children with disabilities (based on specific criteria and implemented according to state laws). In 1986 Public Law 99-457 was passed, which included Part H, the Handicapped Infants and Toddlers Program. Part H addressed the needs of infants from birth through the third birthday. This law mandates the identification and provision of services for infants suspected of being at risk for developmental delay. Eligibility for services usually requires an infant assessment that documents delays (criteria vary across states) in cognitive, physical, communication, social or emotional, or adaptive development, or the infant must have a diagnosed physical or mental condition that is likely to result in developmental delay. The Individuals with Disabilities Education Act (IDEA) extends the provisions of previous amendments to provide additional services to children with disabilities. Information on the criteria for eligibility is available through the Office of Special Education Programs.

INFANT ASSESSMENTS

There are a number of infant developmental assessments on the market today. The following is a brief overview of commonly used instruments that assess children within the first 3 years of life. More extensive reviews that critique the psychometrics of the instruments are provided by Aylward (1994), Kamphaus (1993), and Sattler (1992). The quality of the normative data on these assessments is variable. Although some tests have normative data based on nationally representative samples of children, in other cases, there are no normative data or the normative data are out of date. Before selecting an infant test, readers are encouraged to review the test manuals that accompany the tests to review the procedures used to develop each test, including the establishment of norms. Commonly used infant assessments include:

Battelle Developmental Inventory (Newborg, Stock, Wnek, Guidubaldi, & Svinicki, 1984)

Bayley Infant Neurodevelopmental Screen (Aylward, 1995)

Bayley Scales of Infant Development (Bayley, 1969, 1993)

Brazelton Neonatal Behavioral Assessment Scale (Brazelton, 1973, 1984; Brazelton & Nugent, 1995)

Cattell Infant Intelligence Test (Cattell, 1940)

Clinical Adaptive Test/Clinical Linguistic Auditory Milestone Scale (Capute & Accardo, 1996a, 1996b)

Denver Developmental Screening Test (Frankenburg & Dodds, 1967; Frankenburg, Goldstein, & Camp, 1971; Frankenburg, Fandal, Sciarillo, & Burgess, 1981)

Gesell System of Developmental Diagnosis (Gesell, 1925)

Griffiths Developmental Scale (Griffiths, 1967)

Infant Psychological Development Scale (Uzgiris & Hunt, 1975)

Milani-Comparetti Neurodevelopmenal Screening Examination (Milani-Comparetti & Gidoni, 1967)

The Gesell Developmental Schedules and the Cattell Infant Intelligence Test are the oldest assessments on the list. Although they have historical significance, they are rarely used today because they have been replaced by newer assessments. The Griffiths Developmental Scale was developed and published in Britain over 30 years ago. Infant researchers have been attracted to the Griffiths Scale because it yields scores in six areas of functioning: Locomotor, Hearing and Speech, Eye and Hand Coordination, Performance, Practical Reasoning, and Personal-Social. However, item coverage is very limited and norms are dated.

The Brazelton Neonatal Behavioral Assessment Scale (NBAS) is a newborn assessment that is used by physicians, psychologists, nurses, and physical and occupational therapists to describe the individual differences in information processing and regulation displayed by newborns. Administration is limited to the 1st month of life. The NBAS has been widely used in research and practice and has contributed significantly to our understanding of newborn behavior.

The Denver Developmental Screening Test (DDST) is widely used in primary care settings to screen the development of infants and young children (birth through age 6). It has been revised several times; the most recent revision is the Denver II (Frankenburg, Dodds, Archer & Bresnick, 1990, 1992). One of the strengths of the DDST (and the Denver II) is the one-page record form that highlights the infant's successes and failures, providing a summary of the child's skills at a glance. The Denver II is a screening test, not a diagnostic test. The test has been found to have high sensitivity (proportion of children with developmental problems who are identified), and low specificity (proportion of children without developmental problems who are categorized as normal) (Glascoe, Bryne, Ashford, Johnson, Chang, & Strickland, 1992). Although the Denver II does an excellent job of identifying children who are at risk for developmental delay, the rate of false positives is high. Thus children with developmental delays are not missed, but many children who are developing within normal limits may be identified as suspect. The Denver II is usually followed by a more comprehensive test of infant functioning, such as the BSID-II.

The Clinical Adaptive Test/Clinical Linguistic Auditory Milestone Scale (CAT/CLAMS) (Capute & Accardo, 1996a, 1996b) is a screening test of language, problem-solving abilities, and visual-motor skills for children under 36 months of age. The test has been found to have variable rates of sensitivity (5% to 67%) (Macias et al., 1998; Rossman et al., 1994), and high rates of specificity (95 to 100%) (Macias et al., 1998; Rossman et al., 1994). In contrast to the Denver II, the CAT/CLAMS may miss children who have developmental problems, but the test is unlikely to identify a child who is developing within normal limits as having a developmental problem.

The Bayley Infant Neurodevelopmental Screener (BINS; Aylward, 1992) examines the neuropsychological development of infants from 3 to 24 months of age. It includes items that have been extracted from existing tests and requires approximately 10 minutes to administer. Initial comparisons with other measures of infant development suggest that the BINS has high sensitivity, meaning that it recognizes infants who have developmental delays (Macias et al., 1998).

The Infant Psychological Development Scale is based on Piaget's sensorimotor stage of development (Uzgiris & Hunt, 1975). Unlike many of the other infant tests, it is theoretically based and not norm referenced. It provides a description of the infant's progress in eight areas (Object Permanence, Use of Objects as Means, Learning and Foresight, Development of Schemata, Development of an Understanding of Causality, Conception of Objects in Space, Vocal Imitation, and Gestural Imitation) and is useful in planning interventions.

The Milani-Comparetti Neurodevelopmental Screening Examination (Milani-Comparetti & Gidoni, 1967) examines neuromotor function from birth through 24 months. It is a brief test that can be administered in about 5 minutes and incorporated into a physical exam.

The Batelle Developmental Inventory (Newborg et al., 1984) evaluates children's development in five areas (Cognitive, Communication, Motor, Adaptive, and Personal-Social). The test extends from birth through 8 years of age and includes structured assessment, observation, and caregiver report. The Battelle has become a popular test because it addresses the developmental areas for assessment required by IDEA, includes standardized adaptations for children with disabilities, and includes a screening test that requires 10 to 30 minutes.

A summary of these tests is provided in Rapid Reference 1.1.

≡ Rapid Reference

1.1 Summary of Infant Assessments

Test Title	Source	Age Range	Content Areas
Battelle Developmental Inventory	Newborg et al. (1984)	1 month– 8 years	Cognitive, Personal-Social, Adaptive, Motor, Communication
Bayley Infant Neurodevelopmental Screener	Aylward (1992)	3–24 months	Neurological, Receptive, and Expressive Functions, Processing, and Mental Activity
Bayley Scales of Infant Development	Bayley (1969, 1993)	BSID: 2–30 months BSID II: 1–42 months	Mental, Motor, and Behavior
Brazelton Neonatal Behavioral Assessment Scale	Brazelton (1973, 1984); Brazelton and Nugent (1995)	Birth–1 month	Habituation, Orientation, Motor Performance, Range of State, State Regulation, Autonomic Regulation, Abnormal Reflexes
Cattell Infant Intelligence Test	Cattell (1940)	2–30 months	Cognitive
Clinical Adaptive Test/Clinical Linguistic Auditory Milestone Scale (CAT/CLAMS)	Capute and Accardo (1996a, 1996b)	Birth–36 months	Language, Problem Solving, and Visual-Motor Skills
Denver Developmental Screening Test	Frankenburg (1967); Frankenburg, Dodds, Archer, and Bresnick (1990); Frankenburg, Fandel, Sciarillo, and Burgess (1981); Frankenburg, Goldstein and Camp (1971)	Birth–6 years	Gross Motor, Language, Fine Motor-Adaptive, Personal-Social, Behavior

Test Title	Source	Age Range	Content Areas
Gesell Developmental Schedules	Gesell (1925); Gesell and Amatruda (1941); Knobloch, Stevens, and Malone (1980)	Original: 4–60 months Revised: 1 week –36 months	Adaptive, Gross Motor, Fine Motor, Language, Personal-Social
Griffiths Developmental Scale	Griffiths (1967)	1–60 months	Locomotor, Hearing and Speech, Eye and Hand Coordination, Performance, Practical Reasoning, Personal-Social
Infant Psychological Developmental Scale	Uzgiris and Hunt (1975)	2 weeks– 2 years	Object Permanence, Use of Objects as Means, Learning and Foresight, Development of Schemata, Development of an Understanding of Causality, Conception of Objects in Space, Vocal Imitation, Gestural Imitation
Milani-Comparetti Neurodevelop-mental Screen-ing Examination	Milani-Comparetti and Gidoni (1967)	Birth–24 months	Neuromotor Function

THEORETICAL FOUNDATION OF THE BSID

The BSID represents the lifetime work of Dr. Nancy Bayley and has its basis in the California First-Year Mental Scale (Bayley, 1934), the California Preschool Mental Scale (Jaffa, 1934) and the California Infant Scale of Motor Development (Bayley, 1936). These instruments were developed as standardized assessments of infant development that would produce a score. When the BSID was published it sampled the widest array of mental and motor abilities on a developmental assessment at the time. Bayley included the Infant Behavior Record to account for behavioral aspects of the infant that affect cognitive performance, such as the infant's motivation and quality of interaction with others.

Bayley began work on the California First-Year Mental Scale at the Institute of Child Welfare at the University of California at Berkeley in the 1920s. She incorporated many items from Gesell's assessment and also from other's work such as Kuhlman's (1922) *Handbook of Mental Tests* and Preyer's (1882) *Die Seele des Kendes.* She also developed new items (Bayley, 1933). The BSID was considered to be a theoretically eclectic assessment that borrowed from different areas of research and examined higher functioning (Aylward, 1997).

History and Development of the BSID

The BSID was published in 1969 by a major test publisher, the Psychological Corporation. The test assesses infants between the ages of 2 and 30 months of age. The items are arranged in ordinal sequence of increasing difficulty, representing the maturation of abilities in cognitive and motor development. Raw scores are converted to standardized scores (mean = 100, standard deviation = 16) through tables, yielding a Mental Developmental Index (MDI) score from the Mental Scale and a Psychomotor Developmental Index (PDI) score from the Motor Scale. The Infant Behavior Record provides a description of the infant's behavior in reference to behavior expected of same age infants.

Items from the three California scales, along with newly created items, were piloted in research studies from 1958 to 1960. These studies were funded by the National Institute of Neurological Diseases and Blindness. A second wave of research was conducted by the National Institutes of Health, along with other agencies, beginning in 1960.

The first revision of the BSID, the BSID-II (Bayley, 1993) was designed to update the normative data, to expand the age range to 1 to 42 months, to incorporate research-based items that demonstrate predictive validity, to update the stimulus materials, to conduct reliability and validity studies, to report data from clinical populations of children, and to ensure a standardized assessment of children's mental and motor performance (Rapid Reference 1.2). The BSID-II maintains the same structure as the BSID with Mental and Motor Scales and a rating of the child's behavior, the Behavior Rating Scale (BRS) (Don't Forget 1.1). Like the BSID, the BSID-II Mental Development Index and Psychomotor Development Index have a mean of 100. The standard deviation was changed to 15 (instead of 16 as it is for the BSID) in keeping with most other assessments of cognitive performance.

DON'T FORGET

1.1 Scales of the BSID-II

- Mental Scale
- Motor Scale
- Behavior Rating Scale

≡ *Rapid Reference*

1.2 Goals of the Revision of the BSID

- Update the normative data.
- Expand the age range from 1 to 42 months of age.
- Improve content coverage using research-based items with demonstrated predictive validity.
- Modernize items using materials that facilitate infection control, reduce gender and racial bias, and are attractive to young children.
- Conduct reliability and validity studies and explore the factor structure of the Mental and Motor Scales and the BRS.
- Collect data on clinical populations of children.
- Maintain the primary structure and purpose of the BSID, which is to provide a standardized assessment of infant mental and motor performance based on the infant's response to a structured set of stimulus materials.

The BSID-II, like the BSID, provides overall standard scores for mental and motor development. Although some attempts were made in the revision to provide more comprehensive coverage of all mandated areas of assessment (cognitive, language, social, self-help, and motor), the BSID-II was not designed to provide reliable, valid scores in all five of these areas. The notes made in Caution 1.1 should be heeded, or the BSID-II may disappoint the examiner and referral source if more diagnostic information is sought.

A revision of the norms on the BSID was needed because over time there had been an upward drift of approximately 11 points on the Mental Scale and 10 points on the Motor Scale (Campbell, Siegel, Parr, & Ramey, 1986). This pattern, sometimes referred to as the Flynn effect (Flynn, 1999), has been demonstrated in other cognitive assessments for children and may reflect improvements in nutrition, environmental conditions, and family relations, as well as in our understanding of the determinants of early development. A primary reason for the first revision of the Bayley Scales was to update the norms so they were representative of American children at the end of the 20th century. Therefore *scores obtained on the BSID-II are usually lower than scores obtained for the same children on the BSID.*

This phenomenon should be clarified with parents and colleagues who may misinterpret a child's lower scores on the BSID-II to mean a decline in developmental skills. With the updated norms on the BSID-II, more children

CAUTION

1.1 Design and Limitations of the BSID-II

Feature	Purpose	Limitation
Mental Scale	Produce a standardized score for overall cognitive development; assess higher-order mental processing	Does not provide standard scores for facets or separate domains; does not provide diagnostic information; does not provide standard scores < 50
Motor Scale	Produce a standardized score for overall motor development	Does not provide standard scores for facets or separate domains; does not provide diagnostic information; does not provide standard scores < 50
Behavior Rating Scale	Produce a percentile score for comparison to a nonclinical population; assess behavior related to test-taking session.	Does not provide diagnostic information

should qualify for early intervention services. Remember that the norms for the BSID (and for other developmental assessments that do not have recent norms) are inflated and no longer accurate. The change in the mean scores between the BSID-II and BSID appear in Table 1.1.

The Mental and Motor Scales

The theoretical foundation of the BSID-II remains as eclectic as the BSID. The project staff at the Psychological Corporation, along with various content experts, critiqued the content of the BSID and identified pertinent areas of infant development based on research in the areas of cognitive, language, motor, and personal-social development to be included on the BSID-II.

New items were developed to tap visual and auditory habituation and visual preference in younger infants. In addition, items were added that assess problem-solving abilities including object permanence, perspective taking, and following multistep directions. Many of these items represent higher order cognitive processes, involving reasoning, memory, and the integration of these processes (Aylward, 1997).

Table 1.1   Comparison of the BSID and BSID-II Means for the MDI and PDI

	BSID[a]		BSID-II[b]		Difference	
	Mean	*SD*	Mean	*SD*	Mean	*SD*
MDI	111.6	17.2	99.8	14.9	11.8	2.3
PDI	110.5	15.3	100.4	16.2	10.1	0.9

[a]SD = 16.

[b]SD = 15.

Note. From the *Manual for the Bayley Scales of Infant Development: Second Edition.* Copyright © 1993 by The Psychological Corporation. Reproduced by permission. All rights reserved.

The percentage of language items was increased in the BSID-II because language is a higher order cognitive process that plays a central role in children's cognitive development. The detection of language delay can signal neurological impairment, oral-motor impairment, general cognitive delay, or environmental deprivation. The language items in the BSID-II assess expressive and receptive language as well as grammar usage at the older ages.

Early number concepts and prewriting skills, as well as other items that assess school readiness are included on the Mental and Motor Scales of the BSID-II. A child over 2 years of age is asked to count and exhibit stable number order, one-to-one correspondence, and an understanding of cardinality. Prewriting skills include the ability to rotate the wrist, grasp a pencil, manipulate the pencil, and hold it at the nearest end to draw. Other school-readiness concepts assessed are color identification and discrimination of shape, size, and mass.

Visual perception is assessed by several item types on the Mental Scale with children 2 years of age and older. Tasks vary by the children's age and include matching colors, matching pictures, differentiating objects by size, and discriminating shapes and pictures.

Perceptual-motor integration is also assessed with children over 2 years of age. Children are asked to imitate the examiner's hand movements and body postures on the Motor Scale, and to copy block designs on the Mental Scale.

In the BSID, the item content and coverage of the Motor Scale was particularly weak. Items were added to the BSID-II to assess muscle tone, dynamic and static balance, and perceptual-motor development among the older infants. Items for the younger infants include an assessment of movement symmetry and antigravity movement (Thrusts Arms in Play, Thrusts Legs in Play, Lifts Head When Held at Shoulder, Holds Legs up for 2 Seconds, Balances Head). At the older ages, items assess motor planning and coordination (Swings Leg to Kick Ball, Stops From a Full Run).

Behavior Rating Scale

The BRS is a critical dimension of the Bayley Scales because an infant's state, orientation toward the environment and engagement with people, and motivation may partially explain variations in individual performance on the Mental and Motor Scales. Arnold Sameroff and Ronald Seifer made a significant contribution to the conceptualization and development of the BRS.

The first two items on the BRS are applicable to all infants and are not included in the factors. They represent the caregiver's interpretation of the infant's performance: how typical the infant's behavior was and whether the test was an adequate measure of the infant's skills. These items are very important in the examiner's interpretation of the infant's performance. For example, the infant who has experienced a recent illness, loss, or traumatic event may be more lethargic, less motivated, less cooperative, or have difficulty concentrating and thus may obtain lower scores than under other circumstances.

Items on the BRS are rated on a 5-point scale with behavioral anchors. The items have been factor-analyzed to obtain summed scores for conceptually similar items. The factor structure is somewhat different for the three age groups (1 to 5 months, 6 to 12 months, and 13 to 42 months). In the first age group (1 to 5 months), the BRS assesses Attention/Arousal and Motor Quality. In the second and third age group (6 to 12 and 13 to 42 months, respectively) infants are assessed on Orientation/Engagement, Emotional Regulation, and Motor Quality. Attention/Arousal includes an assessment of the infant's state, affect, energy, interest, exploration, and responsiveness to the examiner. Orientation/Engagement is used for infants 6 months of age and older and includes many of the Attention/Arousal items, along with additional items that assess aspects of the infant's behavior toward the materials. Emotional Regulation is an assessment of the infant's range of affect and emotional response to both success and failure on the assessment. Motor Quality refers to the quality of the infant's movements, including tone and control. Raw scores are converted to percentiles for each factor within each age group. A total raw score can also be converted to a percentile by age group to provide an overall assessment of the infant's behavior.

Item Development

Once new items were written, and some of the remaining BSID items were rewritten for clarification, the items went through three pilot studies, tryout, and standardization. During the pilot studies and tryout, data were collected from approximately 350 and 643 infants, respectively. The developmental sensitivity of each item (i.e., item difficulty according to age of the infant) was evaluated from the data. Ease of administration and appeal to infants

> ### DON'T FORGET
>
> ### 1.2 Changes in Items Between the First and Second Editions of the Bayley Scales
>
> - Old items were dropped (roughly 30%).
> - New items were added (roughly 50%).
> - Some old items were rewritten (in some cases to include a different stimulus, or different administration or scoring directions).[a]
>
> [a]The BSID-II manual lists each new and deleted item. Care should be taken by veteran BSID examiners to note that the instructions for some items that appeared on the BSID have been changed or clarified for the BSID-II.

were evaluated from examiner feedback. During the pilot studies, items were rewritten to clarify administration or scoring, stimulus materials were modified, some items were dropped, and new items were added. After tryout, items were dropped if they were redundant with other items or difficult to administer. Items (along with the stimulus materials) were also revised to reduce racial/ethnic and sex biases. Don't Forget 1.2 lists the types of changes made to the items to facilitate a comparison for veteran Bayley users.

Standardization

The standardization data were collected from a sample of 1,700 infants, aged 1 to 42 months. One hundred infants were in each of 17 age groups (50 females and 50 males in each age group). The ages sampled were in monthly intervals (plus or minus 1 week) through 6 months of age, 2-month intervals from 8 to 12 months of age (plus or minus 2 weeks), 3-month intervals from 15 through 30 months of age (plus or minus 3 weeks), and 6-month intervals from 36 and 42 months of age. The sample was stratified according to the

1988 update of the U.S. census by race/ethnicity, parent education and geographic region. To be included in the normative sample, infants had to be full term (36 to 42 weeks gestation) with birth weight appropriate for gestational age, have no significant medical complications, no disabilities, and not be receiving treatment or intervention for disabilities.

Item Set Development

Unlike the BSID, the BSID-II has circumscribed item sets. The introduction of item sets is a major conceptual change in the BSID-II and one that has introduced significant concern among examiners (Ross & Lawson, 1997). Rather than thinking of individual items, examiners must think in terms of item sets. Along with the change in item sets came a change in the basal and ceiling rules (Don't Forget 1.3). A major complaint of the BSID was the time that was sometimes required to establish a basal and ceiling of 10 consecutive passes and failures, respectively. In addition, it was difficult for examiners to know where to begin testing. Therefore the scores for infants of the same age were not necessarily based on the same series of items. Item sets were constructed in the BSID-II to overcome these complaints from the BSID.

Item sets are organized by chronological age and include a series of items that increase in difficulty. They overlap such that the item set for age 9 months includes the most difficult items in the 8-month item set and the easiest items in the 10-month item set. Therefore movement among items sets is straightforward and in most cases, introduces only a few additional items. The item sets were designed to be broad enough that in most cases an examiner could establish the basal and ceiling within one item set. Each item set includes scores that are approximately ± 1.5 standard deviations from the mean (approximately 78 to 122). When testing infants with scattered abilities or severe delays, clinical judgment is necessary to determine the initial item set. The use of items sets has been a major criticism of the BSID-II and will be addressed more fully in Chapter 5.

RESEARCH ON THE BSID

There have been hundreds of published studies that have used the Bayley Scales with both nonclinical and clinical samples of children, in clinical and research settings, and as an outcome as well as a predictor measure. Numer-

```
DON'T FORGET
```

1.3 Item Sets and Basal and Ceiling Rules

- There are 22 item sets each for the Mental and Motor Scales designated by infant's age.

- Item sets for the Mental Scale have an average of 27 items with a range of 20 to 36 items. The Motor Scale has an average of 17 items with a range of 14 to 21 items.

- Item sets are listed on page 42 of the BSID-II manual and are demarcated on the Record Forms.

- The Mental Scale basal is achieved when credit is received for at least five items in an item set and the ceiling is achieved when no credit is received for at least three items in an item set.

- The Motor Scale basal is achieved when credit is received for at least four items in an item set and ceiling is achieved when no credit is received for at least two items in an item set.

- If a basal is not achieved within the first item set administered, the examiner must go to the previous item set in an attempt to achieve a basal. The examiner continues in this fashion until a basal is reached.

- If a ceiling is not reached within the first item set, the examiner must proceed to the next higher item set in an attempt to reach a ceiling. The examiner continues in this fashion until a ceiling is reached.

- For most infants the basal and ceiling occur within the same item set, but they may occur in different item sets.

ous investigators have examined the psychometric properties of the BSID or compared it with other infant assessments (e.g., Burns, Burns, & Kabacoff, 1992; Costarides & Schulman, 1998; Gerken, Eliason, & Arthur, 1994; LeTendre, Spiker, Scott, & Constantine, 1992). The BSID has been used with typically developing populations to describe variations in development (e.g., Kopp & McCall, 1982) and with at-risk populations to describe the impact of biological or environmental challenges on children's development (e.g., Arendt, Singer, Angelopoulos, Bass-Busdiecker, & Mascia, 1998; Russell et al., 1998). The Bayley has been translated into multiple languages and adapted for use throughout the world (e.g., Chung, Rhee, & Park, 1993; Godbole, Barve, & Chaudhari, 1997; Phatak, 1993). Caution is warranted in using the BSID in populations that differ from the standardization sample because most investigators have not conducted normative studies on the populations they are using. Therefore some examiners who use the BSID for research purposes report raw scores, rather than relying on U.S. norms (e.g., Sigman, Neumann, Carter, Cattle, D'Souza, & Bwibo, 1988).

COMPREHENSIVE REFERENCES ON THE BSID-II

The response to the BSID-II in the research literature has been generally positive, and there is an emerging methodological literature on the BSID-II. The introduction of the BSID-II was met by a series of methodological comments regarding changes in the administration procedures, particularly as applied to premature infants and infants with developmental delays. Nellis and Gridley (1994) provide a comprehensive review of the changes in the BSID-II, together with recommendations for examiners and for subsequent revisions. For example, they suggest that examiners laminate the Cue Sheets so they can be used repeatedly. They also suggest that the manufacturer provide separate technical and administration manuals, rather than combining them into one manual; that there be better empirical support for the facet scores; and that norms be developed to describe development among children with index scores below 50.

The use of item sets has raised many questions. In a study involving 12-month-old infants who had been exposed to cocaine prenatally, Gauthier, Bauer, Messinger, and Closius (1999) illustrate how scores vary depending on the item set administered. Most infants (94%) met basal and ceiling criteria in the 11-, 12-, and 13-month item sets. Regardless of their chronological age, infants who received the 13-month item set achieved higher MDI and PDI scores than infants who were tested on the 11- or 12-month item sets. The authors recommend that examiners apply consistent rules (as recommended in the BSID-II manual) of starting to test with the chronological age item set. Other investigators have also raised concerns on the use of item sets with premature infants (Ross & Lawson, 1997) and infants with developmental delays (Washington, Scott, Johnson, Wendel, & Hay, 1998). Matula, Gyurke, and Aylward (1997) discuss the concerns raised by examiners and emphasize that the BSID-II norms apply only when the examiner adheres to standard administration procedures. Yet examiners can also use the BSID-II to test beyond the item sets to describe the infant's strengths and weaknesses.

Several investigators have compared the BSID and the BSID-II (Goldstein, Fogle, Wieber, & O'Shea, 1995; Tasbihsazan, Nettelbeck, & Kirby, 1997). Goldstein et al. tested premature infants at 12 months of age and Tasbihsazan et al. tested healthy infants from 18 months to 27 months of age.

Both teams of investigators found that, as expected, mean scores on the BSID-II were lower than those on the BSID, suggesting that increased numbers of infants may be eligible for early intervention services.

There has been limited work on the BRS. Thompson, Wasserman, and Matula (1996) used two samples and three age groups to examine the factor structure of the BRS. Additional research is needed on the relationship between the BRS and other measures of development. The Infant Behavior Record of the BSID has been a useful clinical indicator of infant behavior (Wolf & Lozoff, 1985) and, with the strong psychometric properties of the BRS, it should be a useful clinical measure.

Rapid Reference 1.3 provides basic information on the BSID-II and its publisher.

≡ Rapid Reference

1.3 Bayley Scales of Infant Development–Second Edition

Author: Nancy Bayley

Publication date: 1993

Scales: Mental Scale, Motor Scale, Behavior Rating Scale

Age range: 1–42 months

Administration time: 30–60 minutes (depending on age of infant)

Qualifications of examiners: Examiners should have training and experience administering and interpreting standardized assessments with infants (from birth through 3.5 years of age). Test administration is more complex than with other standardized assessments because the examiner alters the sequence of items in response to the infant's behavior and performance. Test interpretation is also complex and requires training in infant development, atypical development, and factors that influence behavior and development. Typically examiners have training at the master's or doctoral level and supervised experience, in accordance with guidelines from the American Psychological Association.

Publisher: The Psychological Corporation

555 Academic Court

San Antonio, TX 78204-2498

800-211-8378 (to order by phone)

http://www.psychcorp.com

Price: $838

🔺 TEST YOURSELF 🔺

1. **What is the age range for the normative data on the BSID-II?**

2. **What are the three scales that constitute the BSID-II?**

3. **Which of the following was not a major goal of the BSID revision?**
   (a) to develop additional subtests
   (b) to expand the age range
   (c) to provide more recent normative data
   (d) to improve stimulus materials

4. **Which of the following is a major strength of the BSID-II?**
   (a) Separate standardized scores are provided for cognitive, language, and motor abilities.
   (b) Standardized scores are based on a large sample that is representative of the U.S. population.
   (c) The normative data include a clinical sample.
   (d) Item sets alleviated the necessity for basal and ceiling rules.

Answers: 1. 1–42 months; 2. Mental, Motor, and Behavior Rating Scales; 3. a; 4. b

Two

HOW TO ADMINISTER THE BSID-II

Before administering the BSID-II (or any test), the examiner should understand *why* the test is being administered—that is, what questions will be answered by the results from the test. A test should not be administered unless the examiner has a clear idea of the goals of testing. In most cases, the examiner reviews the goals of testing with the infant's caregiver prior to the administration of the test to ensure that there is no confusion regarding the questions that the BSID-II is (and is not) able to answer.

The BSID-II, like the BSID, is a standardized test. When standardized results are important, the examiner should make every attempt to administer the test as it was administered during standardization. The manual provides standardized directions for administering and scoring each item. Testing infants with the BSID-II is a difficult skill that requires in-depth knowledge of the administration rules of the BSID-II, familiarity with normal infant development and deviations from normalcy, and close attention to both the infant and the caregiver. The examiner paces the administration of the BSID-II to maximize the infant's interest and cooperation within the limits of the administration guidelines.

TEST MATERIALS

The Bayley kit provides most of the materials the examiner needs to administer the test. The few materials that the examiner must provide are listed in Rapid Reference 2.1. These materials were used to standardize the test, and there are particular aspects about the materials that prohibit a substitution. For example, the blocks' size and material affect the infant's ability and ease to pick them up and stack them; the ball in the kit is quite small, and any larger ball

Rapid Reference

2.1 Materials the Examiner Provides

- Stairs (three steps that are 6½ inches high, 10 inches deep, with a width of at least 24 inches)
- 8½" × 11" blank, white, medium-bond paper
- Facial tissue
- Three plastic bags (small)
- Stopwatch

could make the item that requires the infant to kick the ball an easier item. Materials that are lost or broken can be replaced through the publisher.

PREPARATION OF SITE

Prior to testing, the examiner should select a setting that is optimal for the infant. Under ideal conditions the room should be private, without visual or auditory distractions (e.g., no television), and with adequate lighting and temperature control. Although medical examination rooms are often used to administer assessments to infants, the examiner should be aware that a medical environment might elicit fearful reactions from some infants. Homelike furnishings and a child-oriented decor, including a child-sized table and chairs, may help infants and young children feel more comfortable. However, bright colorful pictures on the walls and objects or other toys in the room may be distracting and interfere with keeping the infant's attention on task. Although it may be difficult to test infants at home because there are many uncontrolled variables (e.g., siblings, noise from a television), it is sometimes necessary to conduct assessments in the home. The examiner can organize a home environment to reduce the number of distractions by ensuring that the caregiver understands the reasons for the evaluation and the need for a quiet, private setting. Similarly, it is often necessary to test infants in hospitals and other busy locations. The examiner who is prepared with a Do Not Disturb sign and strategies to ensure as much privacy and as few distractions as possible will have the most success in maintaining the infant's attention.

Outside noises should be taken into consideration when determining whether a testing site is going to be suitable. These noises might come from surrounding offices, an intercom, elevator shaft, and so on. Although older children might be able to block outside noises, infants are often easily distracted. Temperature control is also important because an infant who is hot or cold may become lethargic or fidgety and thereby less able to concentrate on the testing procedure. In addition, there should be access to steps (three steps that are 6-½ inches high, 10 inches deep, with a width of at least 24 inches) and an area at least 9 feet in length (to allow the child to stop from a full run, as required by Motor Item 100).

Most of the items on the Mental Scale and some of the items on the Motor Scale require the examiner and infant to sit at a table. The room should have furniture that is comfortable for the infant. If the infant is able to sit at a table alone, a child-sized table and chairs should be available, with a chair sturdy enough to support the examiner. For an infant who needs to sit in the caregiver's lap, the table should be at a height that is comfortable for the infant. In some circumstances, particularly when testing young infants, the examiner may use a lapboard that can be moved close to the infant for tabletop activities or the infant may be tested while seated in a high chair. Note that the testing surface should be clear of objects that might distract the infant and should not have a lip around the edge that could be used to aid in picking up objects. During the administration of the items on the Mental Scale, the infant should be positioned to provide adequate trunk and head support so that the infant's attention is directed toward the items, rather than toward balancing. To administer the Motor Scale to young infants, the examiner may use a floor mat or an examination table.

Prior to testing, the examiner should place the test materials required for the estimated item set(s) in a convenient location that is not directly within the infant's view (e.g., on a chair, on the floor, or behind the table). Items that are not in use may be retained in the closed test case. Examiners may have several small toys that are not part of the test kit to engage the infant before testing or if the infant needs a break. Toys such as plastic shapes or rattles are appropriate, but they should not be highly attractive or the infant may not want to relinquish them.

PREPARATION OF INFANT AND CAREGIVER

Testing should be scheduled at a time when the infant is not sleepy, hungry, or ill. Caregivers should be informed about the length of testing (approximately 30 minutes for infants less than 15 months of age and up to 1 hour for infants beyond 15 months of age) and should be instructed to bring a snack in case the infant gets hungry. Depending on the setting, examiners may want to be prepared for infants with a supply of diapers, wipes, and snacks (e.g., milk, juice, and crackers).

Prior to the session, the examiner should also ensure that the caregiver understands the reasons for testing and that the caregiver's understanding is consistent with that of the examiner. For example, infants are often tested to determine if they qualify for services, if their development is progressing as expected, or to gather a baseline before a surgical procedure. It is critical that parents understand that infant testing is not necessarily predictive of later cognitive functioning or school achievement. A lack of clarity in the reasons for testing can lead to disappointment and confusion on the part of the caregiver.

Infants often benefit from having their primary caregiver present, but in most other cases there should not be other people present. When scheduling testing, the examiner should ensure that siblings will not accompany the infant and caregiver; the examiner should advise the caregiver to make arrangements for someone to care for the siblings during testing. Unless the caregiver has to hold the infant, the caregiver should sit behind and to the side of the infant, so the infant and caregiver are not in eye contact. The infant and examiner sit at the table.

CAREGIVER RAPPORT

The examiner begins the session with introductions to the caregiver and infant. In the introduction, the examiner reiterates the purpose of testing and informs the caregiver that it is important to obtain a fair estimate of the infant's strengths and weaknesses. The examiner should emphasize that the infant will be asked to perform some tasks that are easy and below his or her age level and will also be presented with tasks that are above his or her age level. The examiner should tell the caregiver that they will discuss testing at the end of the session, not during the session. The examiner should explain that it is necessary to present tasks that the infant cannot complete to obtain an accurate estimate of the infant's strengths not only in solving problems but also in dealing with difficult tasks. The examiner should tell the caregiver to be supportive, but not to interrupt the infant, offer help, or praise the infant excessively. Comments by the caregiver, even if they are meant to be supportive, can be very disruptive to infants. Some items require the caregiver's assistance; the examiner should prepare the caregiver by saying, "I will need your help, but first I need to work with your infant alone. I will let you know when to help." Conversation with the caregiver should be friendly but brief. Most of the examiner's attention should be directed toward the infant, and the examiner should not interrupt testing to interpret results to the caregiver.

The preparation of the caregiver is essential and can prevent disruptions to testing and confusion about the roles of the examiner and caregiver during testing. Most caregivers are concerned about their infant's performance and in some cases, caregivers may try to assist their infants or even to perform the tasks for them. If the examiner has not adequately prepared the caregiver, it can be awkward to interrupt testing to tell the caregiver to be less intrusive. In contrast, caregivers who understand the purpose of testing and their role in being supportive are less likely to interfere. Moreover, if they do begin to interfere, the examiner can quickly remind them of their role without interrupting the entire procedure. In extreme cases in which the caregiver is disruptive or the infant is distracted by the caregiver (and perhaps having a tantrum), it may be necessary to ask the caregiver to leave. Asking a caregiver to leave is a delicate matter that has to be stated in a very objective manner. The examiner might explain to the caregiver that it is best to complete the exam in one session and that if the caregiver stepped out of the room for a short time, the infant might calm down and resume interacting with the examiner.

If there are other observers in the room (e.g., a student), that person should be located behind the infant and told not to interrupt or to interact with the infant or caregiver. Observers who think they are helping by cheering for an infant's correct responses can be very disruptive and withdraw the infant's attention from the examiner and the test situation.

INFANT RAPPORT

The examiner should begin by observing the infant's interaction with the caregiver to detect how the caregiver comforts the infant and facilitates the infant's interactions. The examiner may use this information to facilitate the infant's performance during testing or in the anticipatory guidance that typically follows the administration of the exam. While the examiner is reviewing the goals of the session with the caregiver, smiles should be directed toward the infant. Since infants and young children may be experiencing stranger anxiety and may be more comfortable interacting with a toy than with the examiner (who is usually a stranger), it is often beneficial to begin a session by giving the infant a toy that is not part of the formal BSID-II materials. Infants may require a few minutes to warm up to the examiner, but if too much time is allowed at the beginning of the session, the infant may tire before the entire test is administered.

The infant's internal state also needs to be taken into consideration when testing. If the infant is sleepy, hungry, or sick and therefore not feeling well, the test results may not be valid. The examiner should look for signals of distress from the infant. These signals are often subtle, especially among young infants, and may include gaze aversion, hiccups, yawns, fussiness, irritability, and inattention. The examiner who is busy talking with the caregiver, looking at the test items, or recording responses may miss the infant's signals, thereby increasing the likelihood that the infant will become fussy, irritable, or distracted. The examiner who is able to read the infant's signals early on and deal with potential signs of distress will be more successful in achieving a valid assessment than the examiner who has to deal with an infant who is crying or refusing to participate. When the infant tires of one material (e.g., blocks or Stimulus Booklet), the examiner should move on to another item and return to the original item later in the session.

If the infant's performance has disintegrated and only a few items remain to be administered, the examiner should try to complete the exam. However, if too much time has passed and there are many items left to administer, the examiner should consider rescheduling to assess the balance of the test. If rescheduling is too difficult, the examiner should try to complete the test. If, on the other hand, the caregiver is willing to return and all agree that the assessment is not going to be representative of the infant's skills, the balance of the exam should be rescheduled. Sometimes a brief break or a snack will revitalize an infant. An infant who is hungry should be given a snack. Testing should be resumed as soon as possible after a snack because some infants get sleepy after eating. When an infant is fighting off sleep or the caregiver reports that the infant is not feeling well, the assessment should be rescheduled to obtain a valid score.

EXAMINER RESPONSIBILITIES DURING TESTING

During testing the examiner's primary responsibilities are to maintain the infant's attention and to administer the BSID-II items according to standardized procedures. The examiner has to have an excellent knowledge of the administration procedures because it is impossible to consult the BSID-II manual during testing. The examiner should focus on the infant, administer a series of items, and wait for a brief break to record the infant's responses. During the session, some examiners opt to record brief notes regarding the infant's performance on a copy of the one-page Cue Sheet (found in Appendix C of the BSID-II manual). During a break or at the end of the session, the notes are transcribed and elaborated on the Record Forms. Under ideal conditions the examination may be conducted with two examiners—one to interact with the infant and the second to record the scores. This two-examiner procedure is often used in training but is usually too expensive for routine administration.

The examiner must remain in control throughout the session. The testing situation is novel to infants and young children, and they frequently look to the examiner for cues on how to behave. The examiner's verbal instructions to the infant should be friendly, direct, and succinct. Because infants and young children tire quickly, the examiner must maintain a steady pace. Instructions should be given as commands, (e.g., "Pick up the block") and not as questions (e.g., "Do you want to pick up the block?"). Examiners who use questions rather than commands risk confusing the infant with excess words or dealing with an infant who says "No."

The transition between items can be difficult for infants and young children. Once infants have become acquainted with a new item, it can be difficult to return it to the examiner. The examiner should present a new material in one hand while reaching for the previous material with the other hand. The testing area should be clear of all materials except the specific test item material in use. Infants are easily distracted, and it is unrealistic to expect them to attend to testing if there are attractive materials in view.

Examiners should take care to praise infants and children briefly for their efforts, but not for their correct responses. An infant who has learned to expect the examiner's praises for correct responses will quickly learn that silence or a change in the examiner's behavior signifies a lack of success. Likewise, it can be awkward for the examiner who has repeatedly said something like "That's right!" to come up with an equally enthusiastic comment after the infant has given an incorrect response. At the same time, constant cheering or applause after every response gets tiring, takes unnecessary time, and can be distracting to the infant who is likely to imitate the cheering. An examiner who makes extraneous comments such as "You answered so fast" may inadvertently encourage an infant to respond quickly because infants may interpret the examiner's comment as an endorsement of a speedy response, rather than a correct response. The examiner should give the infant a quick acknowledgment through a smile or a comment (e.g., "Good work") and move to the next item. Extraneous comments should be kept to a minimum. Videotaping testing sessions can be a very effective way for examiners to review their behavior during testing and to develop an interaction style that facilitates infants' performance.

When an infant refuses to perform an item, it is not usually clear whether the infant could not or would not attempt the item. If an infant refuses a specific item, the examiner should move to the next item and return to the refused item later in the session. The examiner should not reinforce infants' refusals by statements or questions such as "Oh, you don't want to look at the book?" One strategy is to move to the next item quickly. Another strategy is to ask the caregiver to assist in the administration.

An infant who is in the process of mastering a task frequently enjoys repeating it to the point of perseveration. For example, infants will frequently persist in stacking blocks even when they may be able to copy other designs. The examiner should be careful not to get into a conflict with the infant. Instead, the item should be removed and reintroduced later in the session.

In each testing situation, the examiner has to consider how the actual testing environment deviates from the ideal and bear this in mind while interpreting the infant's performance. In some instances it will be best to reschedule and possibly make arrangements for another test site. Rapid Reference 2.2 provides a list of the variables to consider when testing with the BSID-II.

Ultimately, the examiner's clinical judgment is used to decide if the test

≡ *Rapid Reference*

2.2 Important Elements of a Valid Assessment

- Use a complete set of standardized materials (provided in the BSID-II kit, plus the items provided by the examiner). Materials in the estimated item set(s) should be organized and not within the infant's view.

- For younger infants: Provide table and chairs for the caregiver and examiner. The caregiver may hold the infant. Be sure the infant is seated comfortably and can reach the tabletop. Alternatively, a lapboard may be used or the infant may be seated in a high chair. For the Motor Scale, a floor mat or an examination table may be used.

- For older infants: Provide a child-sized table and chair, positioned so that the infant can reach the tabletop comfortably. The additional chair should be sturdy enough for the examiner. The caregiver should be positioned behind and to the side of the infant in a chair. Other observers should be seated behind the infant.

- Assessment should take place in a quiet room without anything that could be visually or aurally distracting. The testing room should be of a comfortable temperature. Ensure that there is access to stairs and an area large enough for an infant to run and jump (at least 9 feet).

- The infant being assessed should be content (i.e., not tired, hungry, or sick).

- Avoid testing in a room where medical procedures have been performed (potentially distressing).

- Avoid having additional people in the room (another adult or sibling) who are distracting.

results are valid (see Chapter 4 for a discussion of how to interpret the validity of the assessment). See rules of thumb for rescheduling listed in Rapid Reference 2.3 (on page 30).

ORDER OF ADMINISTRATION

Items on the Mental Scale are usually administered prior to items on the Motor Scale. Ideally, the session begins with the infant seated and the examiner introduces all the items on the Mental Scale and the tabletop activities on the Motor Scale. Once the infant is asked to get up from the table to perform the gross motor activities on the Motor Scale, it is often difficult to return to

≡ Rapid Reference

2.3 Guidelines for Rescheduling an Assessment

• Consult with the caregiver regarding optimal testing conditions. For example, if the infant is ill, wait until the illness has resolved. If the infant is reported to be more cooperative in the presence of a specific caregiver (e.g., parent rather than grandparent), try to reschedule when that caregiver is available.

• Reschedule as soon as possible, before the infant advances to a higher item set.

• At the second testing, do not repeat items for which the infant received credit. Administer items that were not previously administered or that were refused during the first administration. Items that were attempted and failed during the first administration should not be repeated.

• If the infant exhibits persistent behavior problems, necessitating a referral to a behavioral specialist (e.g., clinical child psychologist), it may be necessary to wait until the behavior problems have resolved before a valid BSID-II assessment can be obtained.

• In the report, indicate that the evaluation was conducted over two sessions and the reasons for the second session.

the sedentary tabletop activities. However, when an older infant does not want to sit at the table from the start of the exam, the examiner may test the child seated on a mat or alter the presentation of the items to introduce motor items prior to tabletop activities.

The Cue Sheets provide a suggested order of administration within each item set. Items that share materials are grouped together to facilitate administration. However, examiners are not bound to the order presented in the Cue Sheets and should modify their order of administration to meet the needs of the infants they are testing. Many examiners copy the Cue Sheets and use them as a guide during testing. They are brief and include all the mental and motor items within a particular item set on one page.

PROVIDING FEEDBACK TO THE CAREGIVER

The testing session provides a rare opportunity for caregivers to watch their infant perform multiple tasks in a very structured setting. Many caregivers are surprised by their infant's capabilities. As soon as the formal testing has been completed, the examiner should ask the caregiver the first two questions on the BRS that address how typical the infant's behavior has been and whether the infant has performed as well as can be expected. These questions give the caregiver an opportunity to explain events that may have adversely affected the infant's performance, such as a recent loss or illness, and provide the examiner with a better understanding of the infant's behavior at home. This information should be incorporated into the interpretation of the results.

Caregivers are often anxious to know how their infant performed, yet examiners must be very cautious about providing results prematurely. Results should not be given to caregivers until examiners have completed the BRS, scored the Mental and Motor Scales, and reviewed the infant's performance in light of referral information or, in the case of an interdisciplinary evaluation, findings from other disciplines. The examiner can comment on the infant's behavior (e.g., "She worked very hard"), but should be very careful not to make general statements on the infant's performance before calculating the scores. A seemingly innocuous comment such as "She did really well" can be confusing to a caregiver who subsequently learns that the infant received a score in the deficient range.

The conclusion of the testing session is an ideal time for examiners to provide anticipatory guidance to caregivers by commenting on emerging skills or skills that the infant exhibited. For example, an examiner may suggest stacking blocks for an infant who is fascinated with blocks or learning to stack them. For an infant who enjoyed looking at pictures, the examiner may model reading a book and suggest that the infant may enjoy reading a book with the caregiver. Examiners may also comment on optimal ways to involve infants in learning activities (e.g., many infants learn through imitation rather than through verbal instruction). This feedback to caregivers focuses their attention on the positive aspects of the infant's performance, regardless of the actual scores.

The examiner should complete the Record Forms of the Mental and Motor Scales and the BRS. The examiner should refer to the BSID-II manual during scoring to ensure that the items are scored correctly. The scoring should be completed as soon after testing as possible, while the examiner's recollections are clear, and certainly before another infant is tested. Once the exam has been scored and the results have been integrated with other findings, the examiner can meet with the caregiver to provide the results, interpretation, and recommendations.

POST-TESTING PROCEDURES

After testing ends, the examiner records final notes regarding the infant's performance and the testing session. In most cases, the examiner prepares a written report that reviews the infant's performance and provides recommendations for services or follow-up. If a referral is warranted, the referral should be made as soon as possible.

The examiner should wash items that the infant has touched, particularly those that have gone into the infant's mouth. An antibacterial cleanser or a solution of one part bleach to 10 parts water is recommended. Items should be returned to their place in the test kit to ensure that nothing is missing and that the test kit is ready for the next administration of the BSID-II.

TESTING INFANTS WITH SPECIAL NEEDS

The BSID-II is often used to test infants and young children with special needs. In many cases, the BSID-II can be administered to infants with special needs with no adaptations. However, adaptations may be necessary to test infants and young children with special needs, such as those who are visually impaired, hearing impaired, or who have limited motor control. Once adaptations are made to the administration of the BSID-II, it is no longer valid to use the norms because adaptations may alter the difficulty of the items. In the report prepared after testing, the examiner should record any adaptations made to the standardized testing procedure. Although it may not be appropriate to provide a standardized score, the examiner may be able to describe the infant's performance at the item level, as well as the infant's performance when adaptations are made.

The BSID-II may be used to evaluate infants and young children with mental retardation. However, the standardization sample does not include norms for infants with a standardized score less than 50. For infants who are significantly delayed and obtain scores below 50, a developmental age equivalent can be reported, performance at the item level can be used to describe the infant's abilities, or extrapolated scores can be used (Robinson & Mervis, 1996). Caution should be taken in using extrapolated scores because they are based on statistical derivations, and have not been empirically validated. However, they can be useful in describing the progress among infants with significant delays. Performance on the BSID-II may be the best means of assessing the abilities of older children (i.e., older than 42 months) with mental retardation. Although the norms cannot be used if children are older than those in the standardization sample (i.e., beyond 42 months), the item performance and the age equivalent scores may be useful.

When an infant's disability does not interfere with the performance of most items, a score can be derived and the examiner should note that performance on certain items was impaired due to the infant's special condition. For example, an infant with strabismus may have difficulty stacking blocks or difficulty visually focusing on other test materials. In this case, the examiner can still obtain an overall MDI and note that the infant has difficulty focusing on small objects because of the strabismus. An infant with cerebral palsy may do well on the mental items that do not have a motor component but may have difficulty on motor items and on mental items that require motor coordination. In this case, the PDI may accurately reflect the infant's abilities, but the MDI would only be accurate if the motor requirements were not affected by the infant's physical limitations.

When the purpose of testing an infant is to document under what conditions or with what adaptations the infant is able to successfully perform an item, the BSID-II item sets can be used as a guide, but a standardized score cannot be derived, nor should a developmental age equivalent be reported. For example, if an infant has difficulty picking up small objects, the examiner may substitute larger blocks for those provided in the BSID-II kit to determine whether the infant is goal oriented, able to stack and release multiple blocks, and can plan how to balance blocks to build a tower. In this situation the infant's performance may be documented and described for the purposes of developing a curriculum for intervention, or evaluating the infant's progress.

A description of the infant's performance (rather than a standardized score) may also be the best an examiner can provide when testing an infant with behavior that is so problematic that it interferes with the assessment. A standardized score or developmental age equivalent may be reported if there are only a couple of refusals. With infants who have severe behavior problems, it is often advisable not to report a score since the infant's mental and motor abilities cannot be accurately assessed given the infant's behavior. In the case of persistent behavior problems, rescheduling the exam is not likely to result in a more valid score since the infant's behavior will most likely interfere again. The examiner will have to use descriptions and clinical judgment in reporting the infant's performance, given the purpose of the assessment and use of the scores.

The BRS is particularly useful when assessing infants with special needs. In many cases a Non-Optimal or Questionable score on the BRS can help explain poor performance on the Mental or Motor Scale or add important information that is not reflected in the MDI or PDI. Specifically, while the infant might be able to compensate for a motor disability while performing some of the items on the Motor scale and receive credit for an item, the Motor Quality Factor on the BRS will reflect any awkward posturing, for example, that the infant displays. An infant who refuses to perform many items and is not responsive to the examiner or the parent is going to have a Non-Optimal or Questionable score on the BRS Emotional Regulation factor or Orientation/Engagement factor or both.

TESTING INFANTS WITH BEHAVIOR PROBLEMS

Infants with behavior problems are often referred for developmental assessments to determine whether their behavior problems are associated with delayed development. In these situations it is critical for the examiner to be extremely familiar with the test items so the examiner's attention can be directed toward managing the infant's behavior.

The items should be administered quickly in a friendly, no-nonsense manner, demonstrating the tasks in question, and ignoring inappropriate or refusal behavior. Begging the infant "Don't you want to stack the blocks" or commenting on the infant's inappropriate behavior or refusals are unlikely to result in the infant's compliance. If the infant persists in throwing items, such as the blocks, they should be removed quickly and reintroduced later in the test session. If the infant has difficulty with transitions and refuses to relinquish a test item even though the next item has been introduced, the examiner can often proceed to the next task and quickly pick up the previous item when the infant's attention is diverted.

Although many infants behave better in the presence of their caregivers, involving the caregiver in managing the infant's behavior during the test session results in mixed success. Some caregivers respond to their infant's inappropriate behavior by yelling or threatening, strategies that often increase the infant's irritability and lead to a tantrum. Other caregivers can redirect the infant to the test session without escalating their inappropriate behavior. In either case the examiner should maintain control of the session and ensure that the caregiver only intervenes at the request of the examiner.

Some infants are extremely shy and will not engage with the examiner. After repeated attempts to gain the infant's confidence, the examiner may ask the caregiver to administer some of the items. Although this procedure is at variance with the administrative rules of the BSID-II, having the caregiver administer test items may yield valuable information on the infant's skill level. The norm tables may be used to calculate scores as long as the caregiver has not deviated far from the standardized procedures.

The examiner can also design the testing area to facilitate compliance. For example, the examiner can position the infant's chair so that it is difficult for the infant to get up or to run out of the room. If an infant persists in getting out of the chair, the examiner can ask the caregiver to hold the infant, although the infant might refuse this option.

Some examiners use behavioral strategies, such as food reinforcers, to increase compliance among infants with behavior problems. As with any behavioral program, this strategy should be implemented with caution and with the agreement of the caregiver. The reinforcers should be small, valued by the infant, and not disruptive to the testing session. It should be given for compliance, not for a correct response.

Some infants have behavior problems that are so severe that it is not possible to administer the BSID-II under any condition. In these situations the examiner may use the items in which the infant was compliant to describe the infant's skills, or if the examiner thinks the infant may perform better during a subsequent test session, the infant may be rescheduled. Sometimes testing should be deferred until the infant has been evaluated or treated by a behavior specialist.

WHEN TESTING BEGINS BELOW CHRONOLOGICAL AGE

Prematurity is defined as a gestational age of less than 37 weeks. When testing an infant who was born prematurely, many examiners correct for prematurity within the first 6 months by subtracting the number of weeks the infant was born early from the infant's chronological age, as indicated on the Record Forms. However, caution is warranted because there has been a great deal of debate about the implications of correcting for prematurity (Kraemer, Korner, & Hurwitz, 1985). With infants who are older than 6 months, examiners vary in how much and for how long they correct for prematurity. Correcting for prematurity can make a substantial difference in scores among young infants, but becomes less meaningful among older infants. For example, if scores were corrected for a 6-month-old infant who was born at 32 weeks gestation, the examiner would use a 2-month correction and begin testing with the 4-month item set. If the same infant were evaluated at 25 months of age, a 2-month correction would have less meaning. Examiners must be careful because applying a correction may inflate an infant's scores and render the infant ineligible for services. Conversely, not correcting may yield unrealistically low scores and cause unnecessary concern within the family. Each examiner makes the decision about correcting for prematurity according to the reasons for testing, the degree of prematurity, and research relevant to prematurity (see Aylward, 1997, for discussion). When testing premature infants, it is essential that examiners report whether they have corrected for prematurity or not. Some examiners report both corrected and uncorrected scores.

Aside from adjusting for prematurity, there are other reasons that an examiner might consider beginning with an item set that is below the infant's chronological age. The examiner may begin with an item set below the infant's chronological age if previous test scores indicate that the infant is significantly delayed, or if the infant has a chronic illness, congenital problem, or disability that is associated with significant developmental delay. However, the examiner needs to be very cautious about beginning at a lower item set. If the infant has splinter skills and could establish a basal by obtaining credit for five of the items in his or her chronological-age item set, the examiner should not start with an item set below the infant's chronological age. Usually, when the examiner does begin testing within the infant's chronological-age item set, only a few items need to be administered before realizing that the infant is performing at a much lower level. The examiner can quickly scan the items to ensure that those with the lowest numbers have been administered (easiest), and then move to the preceding item set.

The caregiver can also be helpful in determining the infant's skill level. For example, the caregiver can confirm whether the infant walks or talks. However, it is not advisable to rely heavily on caregiver report because caregivers are usually not familiar with the particular abilities the examiner is testing. Once the examiner begins testing, it is usually easier to determine where a basal can be established on the Motor Scale than on the Mental Scale.

TIME REQUIRED TO ADMINISTER THE BSID-II

The average amount of time it takes an examiner who is well versed with the item sets to administer the BSID-II is approximately 30 minutes for infants under 15 months of age and approximately 1 hour for infants over 15 months of age. In general, the older the infant is, the longer it takes to administer the items. Most young infants cannot concentrate for more than 1 hour. If the examiner finds that testing requires more than 1 hour, a second session should be considered. Examiners who frequently require more than 1 hour may need

CAUTION

2.1 Preparing for Item Administration

- Calculate the infant's chronological age.
- Determine whether to adjust for prematurity. The decision should be based upon the reasons for testing and any relevant research that pertains to age adjustment and performance for the clinical population the examiner is testing. Full adjustment, especially in young children, may yield scores that are overinflated, whereas no adjustment may yield scores that are unrealistically low.
- Choose the item set that corresponds to the infant's age (chronological or adjusted).
- Be familiar with the item administration and scoring directions for each item in that item set to need only to refer to the item title and to watch for behavior scored on incidentally observed items.
- Regardless of the examiner's decision, the report should indicate whether scores were adjusted for prematurity or not.

to increase the pace of administration. Some of the item sets (e.g., 23 to 25 months) are very long, and the examiner needs to be well prepared to administer these item sets. Testing an infant with behavior problems or one who does not achieve a basal (or ceiling) within the first item set requires more time. See the list of caveats concerning testing time and how to prepare in Caution 2.1.

ITEM SETS

The BSID-II item sets were designed to facilitate ease of administration. The BSID had been criticized because the criteria of 10 consecutive passes for a basal and 10 consecutive failures for a ceiling often made the testing time quite lengthy. In addition, without clear rules on where to begin testing, there was no consistency regarding the items used to establish standardized scores. Thus infants of the same age may have been tested on different items. The introduction of item sets, whereby examiners begin testing infants in the item set that corresponds to their chronological age, was meant to reduce the number of items necessary to establish a basal and ceiling and to ensure that scores for infants of the same age were based on the same set of items. However, the introduction of item sets has been met with confusion and concern (Matula et al., 1997; Ross & Lawson, 1997).

The item sets on the BSID-II were developed according to item difficulty. The first few items in an item set were passed by roughly 95% of the non-clinical, standardization sample. The last items in an item set were passed by only about 10%. The rest of the items were ordered according to item difficulty with some consideration given to ease of administration.

The examiner may verify what items are included in an item set. A list of item sets by age is found on page 42 of the BSID-II manual. The item sets, coupled with the basal and ceiling rules, determine what items should be administered to the infant.

There is much item overlap across ages, for example, a difficult item for a 12-month-old appears as an easy item for a 17- to 19-month-old on the Mental Scale. Therefore the examiner must think in terms of item sets, rather than individual items, when administering the BSID-II. Caution 2.2 offers several suggestions for the examiner when administering the BSID-II.

CAUTION

2.2 Tips for Administering the BSID-II Item Sets

- Highlight on the Record Form the first and last item of the item set you are administering.

- Follow the recommended item order provided on the Cue Sheets in Appendix C of the BSID-II manual. The recommendation is based upon ease of administration, given the test materials that have to be used and the amount of rapport that needs to be built between the examiner and the infant—items that require more examiner-child interaction typically come later. Many examiners photocopy these pages to access during testing and to record notes regarding the infant's performance.

- At the end of the session, complete the Record Forms (Mental Scale, Motor Scale, and BRS).

- Though a particular item may fall within four different item sets, the examiner should consider it only as an item within the item set that is being administered at the time.

- When an infant has received credit for only one or two items and the examiner has administered approximately half of the items in an item set, the examiner may be able to determine whether to continue administering items within that item set or to begin administering items in a previous item set. If the items remaining to be administered are more difficult than items for which the infant has received no credit (e.g., higher numbered items), it is not necessary to administer the later items. The examiner must be extremely cautious in terminating an item set to ensure that the infant is not penalized. The examiner can feel secure in the decision to terminate an item set when the more difficult items tap constructs in which the infant failed easier items. For example, if the infant cannot make a two-word utterance, the examiner can be certain that the infant is not going to say a three-word sentence; if the infant cannot compare sizes, the infant is not going to be able to discriminate among sizes.

BASAL AND CEILING RULES

Along with the new item set configuration, new basal and ceiling rules were established. Given that each item set has a wide range of item difficulty, a basal and ceiling is often achieved within the first item set administered. Don't Forget 2.1 provides the basal and ceiling rules for administering the BSID-II.

When the basal criterion is not met within the first item set administered,

DON'T FORGET

2.1 Basal and Ceiling Rules

	Basal	**Ceiling**
Mental Scale	Five items receiving credit	Three items receiving no credit
Motor Scale	Four items receiving credit	Two items receiving no credit

- Mental Scale basal. The infant must receive credit for at least five items in one item set; otherwise, the examiner must administer all the items in the previous item set. The examiner must continue to drop back to the previous item set and administer all the items until the infant receives credit for at least five items within one item set. (Because of the item overlap across item sets, dropping back to the previous item set usually adds only a few additional items.)
- Mental Scale ceiling. The infant must receive no credit for at least three items in one item set; otherwise, the examiner must administer all items in the next item set. This pattern should be repeated until the infant fails to receive credit on at least three items in one item set and establishes a ceiling. (Because of the item overlap across item sets, administering items from a second item set to establish a ceiling is usually achieved with little additional time).
- Motor Scale basal and ceiling. The same procedure applies to the Motor Scale using the basal and ceiling criteria for the Motor Scale. Basal on the Motor Scale is determined by receiving credit on at least four items within one item set and ceiling is determined by failing to receive credit on at least two items within one item set.

the examiner must go back to a previous item set to establish the basal. Care must be taken in determining the basal and ceiling when more than one item set has to be administered. Caution 2.3 addresses this issue.

RECORD FORMS

Each scale has its own Record Form. Although the Mental and Motor Scale Record Forms were designed to be used exclusively (i.e., without the manual) during test administration, they may be most useful immediately *before and after* test administration. The items on the Record Forms appear in ordinal sequence (to correspond with the order in the manual). However, the item

CAUTION

2.3 Determining the Basal and Ceiling Across Multiple Item Sets

Guidelines

- The basal has to be achieved within a single item set.
- The ceiling has to be achieved within a single item set.
- The basal is established within the lowest item set administered and the ceiling within the highest item set administered. The basal and ceiling do not have to be established within the same item set, although many times they are.

Example

A 12-month-old infant is first administered the 12-month item set on the Mental Scale. The following is the pattern of credits and no credits received for the items within all item sets administered.

12-Month Item Set: Items 71–100	Credit: Items 74 and 75	No Credit: Items 71–73, 76–100	Ceiling
11-Month Item Set: Items 66–92	Credit: Items 67 and 68	No Credit: Items 66, 69, and 70	
10-Month Item Set: Items 64–87	Credit: Item 65	No Credit: Item 64	Basal

Explanation

Within the 10-month item set, the infant received credit for five items (Items 65, 67, 68, 74, and 75). The *basal* was not established until the 10-month item set. If all five of the items for which the infant received credit did not fall within the 10-month item set (i.e., one or more credited items were greater than Item 87), the examiner would have to drop back to the 9-month item set to try to obtain all five items credited within the 9-month item set. The *ceiling* was established within the 12-month item set. Note that even though the ceiling criteria is also met in the 10-month and 11-month item set, the highest ceiling is in the 12-month item set (the item set in which the examiner began testing).

order on the Cue Sheets, which differs from that on the Record Forms, was designed to facilitate administration. On the Cue Sheets, typically all the items that use the same materials are administered together, even though they may vary in item difficulty. Thus, it can be difficult to search for items on the

Record Forms in the middle of the testing session. Examiners may need to review the Record Forms carefully prior to a test session to recall some of the details, such as the number of times a trial is repeated. During the session, the infant's performance may be recorded on a copy of the Cue Sheet. Whenever possible during the session, such as during a break, or immediately after the session, notes from the one-page Cue Sheet can be transferred to the Record Form where the examiner can elaborate on the infant's performance. When necessary, the examiner may consult the Record Form for clarity on administration or scoring during the session, but should do so during a time when the infant is not attempting to solve a task. The examiner who is busy reading the Record Form may miss the infant's performance or risk losing the infant's attention. The examiner is advised to become familiar with the features of the Record Form as quickly as possible. An examiner who uses the BSID-II frequently can become facile with the use of the Record Form alone during testing. Scoring should be verified with the BSID-II manual following testing.

At the end of the session the examiner asks the caregiver the first two questions on the BRS (how typical was the infant's performance and could the infant have done better). The remainder of the BRS is completed after the end of the formal testing session.

Mental and Motor Scale Record Forms

There are 178 items on the Mental Scale and 111 items on the Motor Scale. Each item set is demarcated on the Record Forms with an arrow placed by the first item of the item set and a hand placed beside the last item in the item set. The arrow and hand icon each have the corresponding age noted within or beside the graphic.

The Mental and Motor Scale Record Forms have eight columns. The columns contain information on the following (in order): item number and title, position of infant at the beginning of the item administration, materials needed, next item scored (in series), next item administered (in series), previous item in series, examiner comments and record keeping, and score. The titles of the first three columns are self-explanatory. The fourth, fifth, and sixth columns list items that are conceptually part of the same series. Column four (Next Item Scored) indicates any additional items that can be scored based on the administration of the current item. Columns five and six point to subsequent and previous items in the conceptual series. This information can facilitate item administration and scoring by enabling the examiner to move forward or backward to other items within a conceptual series to gain more information about an infant's abilities. For example, when Item 57 on the Mental Scale is administered (Picks Up Cube Deftly), the examiner can score two other items on the Mental Scale (Items 58 and 65) and two items on the Motor Scale (Items 31 and 37). The previous item in the series is 53 (Reaches for Second Cube). There is no subsequent item in the series. Caution 2.4 sites warnings about items in a series.

> ### CAUTION
>
> #### 2.4 Important Linkages Between Items in Series
>
> - *Next item scored.* The item administration is the same and does not need to be repeated.
> - *Next item administered.* In some cases the next item must be administered next or the item will be spoiled.
>
> Note that the linkages between items in a series are indicated on the Record Forms. The suggested order of item administration in the Cue Sheets corresponds with the linkages.

The seventh column provides space for the examiner to write comments about the infant's performance. Some items in particular require the performance to meet a time limit, or a percentage of correct responses. The examiner should use this space on the Record Form while testing to specify the amount of time it takes an infant to perform the task, or the specifics of the task that the infant was able to accomplish. The examiner may want this information later to verify the scoring of the item against the criteria provided in the manual or to score subsequent or previous items that are similar in administration but have a more or less stringent criteria to receive credit. The last column is provided for entering the score for the item.

BRS Record Forms

There are 30 items on the BRS, each rated by a 5-point scale. The first two items ask for the caregiver's assessment of the infant's performance on the exam and are completed after the exam, but before the infant and caregiver leave. The remaining 28 items are completed by the examiner after the infant and caregiver leave.

The ratings for the items on the BRS are based on the examiner's observations of the infant's behavior during testing. Each item includes an indication of the applicable age range. Be sure to rate only those items that correspond to the age of the infant. Other items should be left blank.

In summary, much practice is needed to become proficient at administering the BSID-II. The manual and Record Form directions are very comprehensive but also very cumbersome.

⚓ TEST YOURSELF ⚓

1. **What materials not provided in the BSID-II kit must the examiner provide?**

2. **Feeding an infant during testing will invalidate the testing.** True or False?

3. **Caregivers should be encouraged to praise their infant following correct responses.** True or False?

4. **Examiners should talk to caregivers during testing, so they understand why the infant is or is not receiving credit for each item.** True or False?

5. **When testing an infant who is suspected of having mental retardation**
   (a) the BSID-II should not be used.
   (b) the BSID-II can only be used if the infant falls in the age range of the test.
   (c) a standardized score cannot be reported.
   (d) a developmental age equivalent can be reported.

6. **When an adaptation is made to the item administration**
   (a) the standard score should be reported.
   (b) the developmental age equivalent should be reported.
   (c) item level scores can be reported.
   (d) the BRS should not be reported.

7. **Items should be administered in the order they appear on the Record Form.** True or False?

8. **The basal and ceiling criteria for the Mental and Motor Scales, respectively, are**

    (a) 5 and 4 credits; 3 and 2 no credits.

    (b) 5 and 5 credits; 3 and 3 no credits.

    (c) 4 and 5 credits; 2 and 3 no credits.

    (d) dependent upon the item set.

9. **The basal and ceiling must occur in the same item set.** True or False?

10. **The examiner should not consult the manual during testing.** True or False?

Answers: 1. 8½" × 11" white, blank, medium-bond paper, stairs, three small plastic bags, facial tissue, stopwatch; 2. False; 3. False; 4. False; 5. d; 6. c; 7. False; 8. a; 9. False; 10. True

Three

HOW TO SCORE THE BSID-II

SCORES PROVIDED BY THE BSID-II

The BSID-II includes three scales: the Mental Scale, Motor Scale, and the BRS. Standard scores (MDI and PDI) can be derived from the Mental and Motor Scales. A developmental age can be obtained from each of these scales as well. In addition, developmental age on facets (Cognitive, Language, Social, and Motor) comprising items from both the Mental and Motor Scales is provided. The BRS yields raw scores and percentiles for two or three factors (depending on the age of the infant), in addition to a total score. Each of these scores serves a somewhat different function. This chapter discusses how to score the scales and the information that is provided by the different scores.

THE MENTAL AND MOTOR SCALES

As discussed in Chapter 1, the Mental and Motor Scales are a compilation of items that are eclectic in terms of underlying theory. The abilities that are represented vary somewhat from item set to item set, according to abilities that should be mastered by a certain age and abilities that are emerging.

Item Scoring

Each item should be scored during administration or promptly afterward based on notations made during the testing. Comprehensive scoring directions are provided for each item in Chapter 4 of the BSID-II manual. Items that have prompted questions and complaints by examiners are addressed in this section. In general, the examiner needs to observe many infants for a wide range of responses before being able to reliably score some of the BSID-II

CAUTION

3.1 Eliciting a Response Versus Teaching An Item

- BSID-II directions were written for the examiner to elicit a response from the infant.
- An infant who has mastered a task can perform it relatively easily.
- An infant who has not mastered a task demonstrates approximations of the required skill.
- When infants are in the process of learning the task (emerging skills), their behavior may be inconsistent—sometimes successful, sometimes not successful.
- Infants performing a task that has been mastered are focused on the task and perform it easily.
- Infants attempting to perform a task above their skill level are likely to display diffuse attention and higher levels of distractibility.
- When more effort is required to elicit a response than provided in the directions, the standardized administration has been breached and the examiner has begun to "teach" the item through repeated administrations, alterations of wording, additional gestures, or encouragement.
- It is often useful for the examiner to drop back to an item from a previous item set to observe the infant's behavior when he or she can easily accomplish a task to contrast with the infant's behavior toward an item that requires a skill not yet mastered.

items. Many times the examiner who tests infants who are developmentally delayed gets the impression that the BSID-II items are extremely difficult for an infant to perform adequately. Assessing normally developing infants from time to time helps examiners understand the simplicity of many of the items and the limited effort that is necessary to elicit a valid response. Cautions 3.1 and 3.2 include guidelines for obtaining a reliable score.

CAUTION

3.2 Reliability of Infant's Response

The examiner should be sure that the infant's response is purposeful. For example, if the infant is manipulating the round puzzle piece and it drops into the appropriate form, the examiner should repeat the item to be sure that the infant's response is intentional.

Mental Scale

Item 26 Habituates to Visual Stimulus
Item 27 Discriminates Novel Visual Pattern
Item 28 Displays Visual Preference
Item 29 Prefers Novelty

These items are in the 2- to 3-month item set and use the visual stimulus cards, easel, and stopwatch. They were adapted from research procedures typically conducted in an experimental laboratory with precise, highly controlled equipment (Fagan, Singer, Montie, & Shepherd, 1986; Fantz & Fagan, 1975). The procedures were adapted for use in a field situation but rely on the examiner's ability to assess the precision and duration of the infant's gaze. Examiners have complained that the procedure is cumbersome and that it is difficult to evaluate infant gaze. With an infant this young, the examiner should sit at a 45-degree angle to the side of the infant to observe the infant's eyes. In this position the infant should gaze at the stimulus cards and not at the examiner. When an infant is attending to a visual stimulus, the entire body is involved in the process (Ruff & Rothbart, 1996). Not only is the gaze fixated on the object, but motor activity is reduced, the infant is not making sounds, and the facial expression is characterized as intense (brows drawn together, no movement in the eye or cheek area, and mouth open and relaxed). A period of attention often ends as infants shift their gaze or their motor activity increases. Examiners often administer these visual items toward the end of the 3-month item set so they have some experience with the individual infant's attention span (i.e., level and duration of attention the infant typically displays, and strategies that are effective in eliciting the infant's attention). Generally, if an infant attends to a stimulus (as opposed to scanning the card or focusing on the edge) it is clear when the infant habituates. Similarly, when an infant discriminates between a novel and familiar pattern or between patterns of varying complexity, it is obvious to the examiner. If the examiner cannot determine whether the infant has been attending or whether the infant has shown a preference, in most cases, the infant has not attended or shown a preference.

Item 63 Imitates Vocalization

The scoring criteria state that the infant should imitate at least one vocalization. The examples given are vocalizations such as "gaga" or "baba." Though not specifically stated, to receive credit the infant should imitate a vowel-consonant sound rather than just a vowel sound. The vowel-consonant combination does not need to be repeated, however; for example, "ga" or "ba" alone should receive credit.

Item 88 Retrieves Toy (Clear Box I)
Item 105 Retrieves Toy (Clear Box II)

When administering Item 105 in the 17- to 19-month item set (the item set does not include Item 88), it is best to administer Item 88 first. The administration of Item 88 adds little time; allows the administration of Item 88 to precede Item 105, as in the administration of the 14- to 16-month item set; and if it is necessary to go back to the previous item set for an infant, it is more efficient to have given Item 88 before Item 105.

Item 108 Points to Three of Doll's Body Parts

Credit is given to the infant who can point to the body parts on a doll that the examiner names. Credit should not be given to the infant who can only point to her or his own body parts (and not to the doll's), as this is an easier task.

Item 144 Discriminates Pictures I
Item 145 Compares Sizes
Item 147 Compares Masses
Item 151 Discriminates Pictures II
Item 156 Understands Concept of More

These items include multiple trials. To receive credit for the item, the infant must receive credit on all trials. Therefore, if the infant does not receive credit for the first trial, technically the examiner could stop the item administration. However, the examiner can gain more information about the infant by administering the subsequent trials; the examiner may observe that the infant "learns" the task after an additional trial.

Item 146 Counts
Item 157 Counts One-to-One Correspondence
Item 159 Counts Stable Number Order
Item 164 Counts Cardinality
Item 175 Counts Order Invariance

These quantitative items can be confusing. To administer Item 146 (Counts), the examiner instructs the child to count but does not present blocks or objects to count. A child receives credit by counting to three: "One, two, three." If the child receives credit for Item 146, Item 164 (Counts Cardinality) is administered immediately. Item 164 examines children's ability to quantify and includes five blocks and two trials. The child must provide the correct response for both trials to receive credit. In the first trial the examiner places the blocks on the table and instructs the child to count the blocks, pointing to the block on the child's left. The examiner then asks the child how many blocks there are. Note that the correct response for this trial is not necessarily "five." The correct response for the first trial is the last number given by the child when counting the blocks. If the child counted the blocks by saying "One, two, four, five, six," then the correct response for the question "How many blocks are there?" would be "Six." If the child answered "Five," the response would not be correct (even though there are actually five blocks on the table). In the second trial, the examiner asks the child if there are *x* blocks on the table where *x* is one more than the number last spoken by the child when counting. The correct response for Trial 2 is always "No." The following example illustrates the confusion that can arise. In the first trial, a child counts the five blocks by saying "One, two, three, four," and the examiner asks, "How many blocks are there?" The correct response is "Four." In the second trial, the examiner asks, "Are there five blocks on the table?" and the correct response is "No." One additional cautionary note: When children's quantitative skills are emerging, they sometimes give answers that are partially correct, or they recognize their errors and self-correct. Thus a child whose quantitative skills are emerging may count "One, two, three, four" and then self-correct by answering "Five" when asked "How many blocks are there?" The skilled examiner recognizes the emerging quality of the child's skills, gathers up the blocks, and begins the task again.

If the child receives credit for Item 164, Item 175 (Counts Order Invariance) should be administered next. With the five blocks remaining on the table, the examiner points to the block at the child's furthest right and says, "If we start counting here, how many blocks will we have?" The child receives credit for reporting the same number as was reported for 164 *without counting*. The examiner should stop the child from counting. Again, "five" is not necessarily the correct response—to demonstrate comprehension of order invariance, the child must repeat the same response as was given for Item 164.

Item 157 (Counts One-to-One Correspondence) can be scored from the administration of Item 164. If Item 164 is not administered, Item 157 can be administered independently. The examiner places five blocks on the table and instructs the child to count them. The child receives credit if he or she assigns only one number to each block; the sequence of the numbers does not matter. Item 159 (Counts Stable Number Order) can also be scored from the administration of Item 146 and Item 164. Credit is received if the child repeats the numbers in the same sequence, even if the sequence is incorrect. Thus a child who counts "One, two, three, four, six" the first time would only receive credit for this item if he or she repeated the same sequence on a second administration.

Calculating the Raw Score

The Mental and Motor Scale Record Forms provide a column in which the examiner can enter each item score. At the bottom of each page of the Record Form, space is provided to sum all credited items on that page. This step facilitates summing all credited items when an item set spans two or more pages.

There are five options (Rapid Reference 3.1) for recording an infant's response to an item: credit (C), no credit (NC), refused (RF), caregiver report (RPT), and omit (O). The only time an infant's response should be given a score of 1 is for a response that receives credit. All else is scored 0. The notations are very useful when writing the report because they enable the examiner to explain specific aspects of the child's responses.

NC is given when an infant performs a task but the performance does not meet the scoring criteria. When a child ignores the examiner during item administration, or otherwise refuses to attempt to perform a task, the examiner can note this as RF. When an infant refuses to perform multiple items, the examiner needs to decide whether to reschedule testing. Testing should be rescheduled if the examiner thinks that the infant's behavior problems are

≡ *Rapid Reference*

3.1 Scoring Options

Score	Criterion	Notation	Points
Credit	The infant's performance on the task meets the scoring criteria.	(C)	1
No credit	The infant's performance on the task does not meet the scoring criteria.	(NC)	0
Refused	The infant refuses to attend to the task or to try to perform the task.	(RF)	0
Omit	The examiner fails to administer the item intentionally or accidentally.	(O)	0
Caregiver report	The caregiver reports that the infant has displayed the behavior or skill at some other time.	(RPT)	0

≡ *Rapid Reference*

3.2 Four Steps for Calculating the Raw Score for the MDI and PDI

1. All items within the item sets administered to establish the basal and ceiling that receive credit (C) are given 1 point.

2. Sum all items that received credit (C) as described in Step 1.

3. Each item below the item set in which the basal is established is credited.

4. Add the items receiving credit from the item set(s) administered (Step 2) to the number of items below the basal item set (Step 3) to obtain the total raw score.

temporary or associated with a specific cause or event (e.g., recovery from illness, initial stranger anxiety). However, if the infant's behavior is likely to be consistent on a 2nd day, the examiner should proceed and not reschedule testing. When an infant does not receive credit for a task, but the caregiver reports that the infant is able to perform the task, the examiner may record RPT. The item will still receive a score of 0, but when writing the report or considering whether the child needs to be referred for intervention, the examiner can note the discrepancy and indicate that the infant may perform better in familiar surroundings. The examiner should never accept a caregiver report in lieu of attempting to administer an item. An examiner may omit an item for various reasons. The examiner may intentionally omit an item when the infant has not passed an easier item and the examiner believes administering a more difficult item would cause the infant more frustration. In addition, items are sometimes omitted due to time constraints, missing materials, or the examiner's forgetting to administer an item. Because omitted items do not receive credit, the examiner should be extremely cautious about omitting items and jeopardizing an infant's score. No more than 10% of all items in the administered item set(s) should receive a score other than C or NC. If many items are refused or omitted, the score should be considered invalid.

Once the appropriate items are administered, the examiner can calculate the raw score according to the steps in Rapid Reference 3.2.

Example 1

The BSID-II Mental Scale is administered to a 6-month-old. The examiner begins testing by administering the 6-month item set. The following provides an example of calculating the raw score.

> *6-Month Item Set: Items 49–73*
> Items Receiving Credit: 49, 51, 52, 54, 55, 56, 59, 60, 61
> Items Receiving No Credit: 50, 53, 57, 58, 62–73

The basal criterion for the Mental Scale (credit for at least five items) is met within this item set. The ceiling criterion (no credit for at least three items) is also met within this item set. In this example, the infant received credit for nine items and received no credit for sixteen items. Thus the raw score is calculated as follows: (a) Items 49, 51, 52, 54, 55, 56, 59, 60, and 61 are given a score of 1; all other items within the 6-month item set receive a score of 0; (b) the sum of all items receiving credit is 9; (c) all items below 49 are credited; and (d) the raw score total is 48 + 9 = 57.

Example 2

The BSID-II Mental Scale is administered to a 7-month-old. The examiner begins by administering the 7-month item set. The basal criterion is not met, and the examiner continues to go back to previous item sets to establish a basal.

7-Month Item Set: Items 54–73
Items Receiving Credit: 55, 56
Items Receiving No Credit: 54, 57–73

6-Month Item Set: Items 49–73
Items Receiving Credit: 49
Items Receiving No Credit: 50–53

5-Month Item Set: Items 42–66
Items Receiving Credit: 42, 43, 44, 45, 46, 47
Items Receiving No Credit: 48

The basal criterion is not reached until the 5-month item set; credit is received for at least five items in this item set. The ceiling criterion is achieved in the 7-month item set; no credit is received for at least three items and it is the highest item set in which the ceiling criterion is met. Thus the raw score is calculated as follows: (a) items 42 through 47, 49, 55, and 56 are given a score of 1; all other items within the 5-, 6-, and 7-month item sets receive a score of 0; (b) the sum of all items receiving credit is 9; (c) all items below 42 are credited; and (d) the raw score is 41 + 9 = 50.

To avoid the most common errors in calculating raw scores, refer to Caution 3.3.

CAUTION

3.3 Common Errors Made in Calculating the Raw Score

- Not following the "lowest basal, highest ceiling" rule and instead giving credit for only those items in the lowest (youngest) item set in which the basal and ceiling criteria are met
- Giving credit for items above the ceiling when the examiner has noted that the infant could perform the task
- Giving no credit for items below the basal when the examiner has noted that the infant could not perform the task

Note. The infant who is unable to complete items below the basal or who successfully completes items above the ceiling is displaying an unusual developmental pattern. The examiner may choose to "test the limits" and note the child's weaknesses or strengths when writing the report. The standard score can be used as long as standardized scoring directions are followed for deriving the total score. When the examiner is not interested in reporting the standard score, the examiner may choose to discuss the strengths and weaknesses and report developmental age for the facets or Mental and Motor Scales.

Obtaining the Index Score

The MDI and the PDI are the most reliable and valid scores in the BSID-II. The scores are placed on the same metric, allowing comparisons between the infant's performance on the Mental and Motor Scales, between scores achieved by one child over two time periods, or between scores achieved by two children.

The BSID-II index scores are a "smoothed," normalized distribution of the standardization sample's raw scores converted to a scale with a mean of 100 and a standard deviation of 15 (the BSID had a standard deviation of 16). The index scores range from 50 to 150 (or +/− 3⅓ standard deviations from the mean). Theoretically, for a normal distribution of a sample's scores, approximately 68% of the scores are within one standard deviation of the mean, 27% of the scores are between one and two standard deviations from the mean, and 5% of the scores are between 2 and 3 standard deviations from the mean. The BSID-II manual reports that the distribution of scores for the standardization sample of the BSID-II closely approximates the theoretical normal distribution. Don't Forget 3.1 provides a description of the normative sample.

DON'T FORGET

3.1 The Normative Sample

- The normative sample is representative of the 1988 U.S. census, according to parents' education level, ethnicity, and geographic region.
- An equal number of males and females are included at each age.
- The normative sample is representative of a nonclinical population so that any infant can be compared to the normal development of her or his same-age peers.

Rapid Reference

3.3 Selecting the Appropriate Norm Table

- Refer to the calculation of the infant's age on the front of the Record Form.
- Each norm table is designated according to the infant's age in months and days (e.g., the 30 Months Norm Table spans from 29 months, 16 days, to 30 months, 15 days).
- The infant's precise age (including days) must be used to select the appropriate norm table for scoring. (For infants born prematurely, a separate decision is made regarding adjustment before testing.)

Once the raw score has been calculated, the examiner turns to Appendix A in the BSID-II manual and uses the Norm Table that corresponds to the infant's (corrected or chronological) age to obtain the index score (MDI or PDI). Rapid Reference 3.3 provides guidelines for selecting the appropriate norm table.

Developmental Age Equivalent of Raw Scores

While the index score (MDI or PDI) provides the most psychometrically sound score, reporting a developmental age in conjunction with the index score is sometimes desired. The developmental age is a direct and simple way to report the infant's performance to a parent or caregiver. In other words, an 18-month-old infant who obtains a raw score of 64 on the Motor Scale would have a PDI of 55, which is classified as Significantly Delayed Performance. Using Table B-2 (p. 325 of the BSID-II manual and reprinted in Table 4.4 on pages 72–73 of this book), the examiner could convert a raw score of 64 to a developmental age of 12 months. Caregivers might find it relatively easy to understand that their infant's motor skills are at a 12-month-level. However, there are at least four cautionary notes in using developmental ages to interpret scores to caregivers. First, caregivers sometimes think that developmental age applies to the infant as a whole. The examiner should emphasize that the developmental age refers only to those abilities assessed with the BSID-II (e.g., motor skills) and not necessarily to other aspects of the infant's development, such as growth, self-help skills, or social maturity. Second, developmental age may be confusing when an infant has a developmental profile that is atypical, rather than merely delayed. For example, the 18-month-old infant with a PDI of 55 who has cerebral palsy and abnormal tone may exhibit motor development that is very dissimilar from a typical 12-month-old. Although the infant has a motor developmental age of 12 months, the caregivers should not be misled into thinking of the child as a typically developing 12-month-old. Third, caregivers may be easily confused by the developmental lag. For example, a child who is 3 months delayed at 12 months of age (developmental age of 9 months) will probably not be 3 months delayed at 24 months of age, but is more likely to be at least 6 months delayed (developmental age of 18 months).

In a final cautionary note, developmental age may be confusing when a child has uneven development. This problem occurs more frequently on the Mental Scale than the Motor Scale because the Mental Scale represents an eclectic combination of cognitive skills, including language skills. For example, a child with cognitive or problem-solving skills in the average range, but delayed language skills will achieve a score on the Mental Scale of the BSID-II that underestimates his or her cognitive or problem-solving skills. Examiners must review the pattern of children's responses to detect these discrepancies and explain them to caregivers (and to colleagues). In this case, mental developmental age would not be particularly helpful because it underrepresents the child's cognitive skills. However, the facet scores might be helpful because they separate cognitive skills from language skills.

Facet Scores

Once the MDI and PDI are calculated, the examiner needs to identify the infant's strengths and weaknesses. The facet scores may facilitate this process to a limited degree, although much caution is required.

The facet scores are divided into four areas: Cognitive, Language, Social, and Motor. Item placement was informed by content experts' classification and item-to-total correlations for each item by facet (as defined by the experts). Given the items on the BSID-II, the strongest facets (item coverage across age groups) are the Cognitive and Motor facets. The Language facet has very few items past 24 months, and the Social facet has very few items past the first few months.

Extreme caution is recommended in using developmental age equivalents on the facets because there is some discrepancy between where an item is placed on the Mental or Motor Scale and where it appears on a facet. This discrepancy is due to the manner in which item difficulty and developmental age were calculated. Item difficulty for items on the Mental and Motor Scales was calculated separately, whereas item difficulty for the items on the facets was calculated with the Mental and Motor items together. The two procedures affect the estimated item difficulty of each item. A second procedure was employed to calculate the developmental age equivalent for the items on the facets once item difficulty was calculated. This additional manipulation of the data altered item placement, sometimes creating discrepancies between placement of items on facets in relation to their placement on the Mental and

Motor Scales. The Mental and Motor Scales are more psychometrically sound than the facets and should be used in interpretation. For example, Mental Item 42 (Reaches for Cube) is the first item in the 5-month item set. This means that it is an easy 5-month item and about 95% of the 5-month-old infants in the standardization sample passed this item. The item is beyond the 3-month item set, meaning that it is a very difficult item for a 3-month-old. In calculating the developmental age equivalent of the Cognitive facet, Mental Item 42 is listed at the 3-month level. If an infant does not pass this item (along with the majority of items placed at the 3-month level), the infant will possibly be placed at a 2-month developmental age on the Cognitive facet. Indeed, the majority of the items at the 3-month developmental age equivalence on the Cognitive facet are very difficult items for a 3-month-old, according to their placement on the Mental Scale. This discrepancy results in a conservative estimate of developmental age equivalence.

Infants With Atypical Development or "Splinter" Skills

The organization of items and item sets is based on the premise that development follows an orderly progression. Thus an infant who passes items at the 11-month level is presumed to be able to pass items designed for infants at the 1- to 10-month levels. For most infants, including those in the standardization sample, this premise is correct. However, the BSID-II is often used with infants who have atypical developmental profiles. There are times when a skilled examiner knows that although an infant has met the criteria for the basal and therefore should receive credit for items in all previous item sets, the infant is unable to complete all the preceding items. Delayed language skills are one example. An infant may reach basal in the 20- to 22-month item set of the Mental Scale by receiving credit for five items, but have no expressive language skills. By the guidelines of the BSID-II, the child should receive credit for all items below the 20- to 22-month item set. However, the skilled examiner who detects the expressive language delay may "test the limits" by administering the expressive language items below the 20- to 22-month item set. The examiner who chooses to "test the limits" by administering items below the 20- to 22-month item set is no longer adhering to the administrative rules of the BSID-II. The examiner may report the MDI or PDI scores if the

≡ *Rapid Reference*
....

3.4 Infants Who Have Atypical Development or "Splinter" Skills

An examiner who suspects that an infant has splinter skills or atypical development and either could successfully perform tasks above the ceiling or could not perform tasks below the basal, may follow a two-step procedure:

1. The examiner should follow the standardized administration to determine the infant's raw score and MDI and PDI.

2. The examiner "tests the limits" by testing below the basal item set or above the ceiling item set to obtain a more complete picture of the infant's skills.

The scores obtained from testing below the basal or above the ceiling may be a more accurate estimate of the infant's skills than the MDI or PDI scores but must be reported using descriptors and developmental age estimates because the examiner has deviated from the standardized administration.

test is scored according to standardization directions and the testing of limits is used only in a descriptive report. In the report, the examiner should clarify how the test was administered. If the examiner does not care to report the MDI and PDI and wants to deviate from standardized scoring, developmental age on the facets and the Mental and Motor Scale may be reported (see Rapid Reference 3.4).

BEHAVIOR RATING SCALE

The BRS is completed by the examiner, based on observations of the infant's behavior during administration of the Mental and Motor Scales. The BRS includes 30 items that are rated on a 5-point scale. The items are listed on seven pages of a Record Form along with each item's scale with behavioral anchors. Space to record the scores is provided on the front of the BRS record form. The first two items of the BRS are questions that the examiner asks the caregiver after the administration of the BSID-II, as noted in Don't Forget 3.2. The first question pertains to the infant's behavior in general and the second question pertains to the infant's ability to perform the BSID-II tasks in comparison to the skills that the caregiver has observed the infant

DON'T FORGET

3.2 BRS Items to Administer to the Caregiver

After the administration of the BSID-II but before the caregiver leaves, ask the caregiver to respond to the first two questions on the BRS: BRS Item 1 (Parental Assessment of Test Session) and BRS Item 2 (Parental Assessment of Test Adequacy). If the examiner has not had the opportunity to observe how the caregiver has to soothe the infant when the infant gets upset during the assessment, the examiner should also ask the caregiver to respond to BRS Item 7 (Soothability When Upset).

demonstrate at home. The examiner may also need to query the caregiver about the infant's ability to be soothed (Item 7 Soothability When Upset), if the examiner does not observe this during administration of the Mental and Motor Scales. The examiner should score the rest of the behaviors as soon as possible after the assessment.

Item Scoring

A brief definition of each behavior is provided in Chapter 4 of the BSID-II manual. A word of caution is advised concerning Items 1 and 2. In some cases it is difficult for the caregiver to understand what information the examiner is trying to obtain. Upon asking the questions, the examiner needs to listen to the caregiver's first response and then ask questions to clarify what the caregiver is saying. For example, with respect to Item 1, if the caregiver says, "This is the way she always acts," the examiner may need to ask if the infant *always* acts this way or *usually* acts this way (sometimes behaves differently) to determine whether to rate the item a 4 or 5. If the caregiver responds, "She always acts this way when she is in new places," the examiner needs to question the caregiver further about the child's typical behavior to determine whether to rate the behavior during testing as somewhat typical (3) or mostly atypical (2) because the infant is rarely in new places. If the infant's behavior was so extreme that the caregiver has never seen the type of behavior that was displayed during the assessment, the item should receive a 1.

When querying the caregiver about the assessment of test adequacy (Item 2), the examiner needs to determine whether the caregiver is comparing the infant's performance on the BSID-II to similar tasks or to other performance such as self-help activities or activities that require no structure (e.g., dancing to music). Unrelated activities may be evoked by a caregiver who is frustrated after an assessment because the caregiver feels that the infant does much more at home. In other instances the caregiver may be unable to distinguish between the infant's ability to label a picture of a shoe, for example, and go and get his shoes when his mother asks him before going out the door. Clarification of the questions to the caregiver and clarification of the caregiver's response will make these two item responses much more meaningful for interpreting the infant's performance and making recommendations.

There are items on the BRS that examiners have had difficulty scoring. The behavioral anchors for some of the Motor Quality items can be confusing because having a certain motor quality all, part, or none of the time is not necessarily an accurate description. For example, hypotonicity or hypertonicity often occurs in specific muscle groups and may be related to positioning. A categorization of how frequently it occurs may not be accurate. Nonetheless, the ratings capture general qualitative differences in Motor Quality that differentiate normal from abnormal, but not necessarily the specifics of abnormalities.

Computing the Factor Raw Scores

The BRS provides scores on separate factors that vary according to the age of the infant, and a total score. For the infant 1 to 5 months of age, a score for Attention/Arousal and Motor Quality can be obtained. For infants 6 to 42 months of age, the following three factors can be scored (though the factors have a somewhat different item composition for 6- to 12-month-olds than for 13- to 42-month-olds): Orientation/Engagement, Emotional Regulation, and Motor Quality.

The examiner must transfer the scores for each item to the front of the record form, where the items are arranged according to age and factor. This is a somewhat tedious and time-consuming task. After transferring the scores, the examiner sums the item scores for each factor. Space is provided on the front of the record form to record the sum. Items 1 and 2 are not included in any of the factor scores or the total score, but they are very useful in determining the validity of the assessment.

DON'T FORGET
....

3.3 Computing the Total Score on the BRS

Item 19 (Orientation to Examiner) and Item 29 (Frenetic Movement) each appear on two factors. When summing across factors to obtain the total raw score, the item scores for these items need to be subtracted once from the total score. This instruction is noted on the front of the BRS Record Form.

Computing the Total Raw Score

The total raw score is the sum of the factor raw scores and additional items (one to two items that did not have a factor loading high enough to be included on any factor). One needs to be aware that when summing the total raw score of the 13- to 42-month-old infants there are two items (Items 19 and 29) that appear on two factors because they had comparable factor loadings on both factors. Although each item score is included in the sum of both factor scores, it should be included in the total score only once. Therefore, when calculating the total raw score, Items 19 and 29 must be subtracted once. For example, if a 15-month-old infant received a 5 on Item 19 and a 4 on Item 29, when the total score is calculated, the examiner should add the scores for the Orientation/Engagement, Emotional Regulation, and Motor Quality factors, together with the additional items, and should then subtract 9 (the sum of scores for Items 19 and 29). The scoring portion on the front of the BRS Record Form has a note to this affect and has shading to highlight the items that are included on two factors. However, the examiner has to be careful because it is easy to forget to subtract the duplicate scoring when summing across the factors for the total raw score (see Don't Forget 3.3).

Percentiles

The scores on the BRS are not normally distributed, but they reflect a distribution of scores expected in a nonclinical population, such as the standardization sample for the BSID-II. The behaviors are rated on a 5-point scale and most of the children in the standardization sample scored a 4 or a 5 (i.e., optimal behavior). The percentiles are provided as a means of detecting scores that only a small percentage of the standardization sample received. An infant whose score is at the 10th percentile or less on any factor is considered to have a Non-Optimal score. A score of 11 to 25 is considered Questionable. Any score greater than 25 is considered Within Normal Limits.

Table B.1 in Appendix B of the BSID-II manual contains the percentiles for the BRS factor scores and total score. The percentiles are listed by factor and age group. Space is provided on the front of the BRS Record Form for recording the percentiles.

🐟 TEST YOURSELF 🐟

1. **Those items that the examiner observes the infant perform or that the caregiver reports the infant can perform are given a score of 1.** True or False?

2. **With respect to an infant's refusal to perform an item**
   (a) the examiner need not worry as this is typical behavior.
   (b) too many refusals can invalidate the assessment.
   (c) the examiner can accept a caregiver report in lieu of the infant's performance.
   (d) the examiner should record this as NC.

3. **A basal and ceiling may be established in two different item sets.** True or False?

4. **When an examiner observes performance on an item below the basal or above the ceiling, these items should be included when calculating the raw score.** True or False?

5. **The MDI and PDI have a mean of 50 and a standard deviation of 10.** True or False?

6. **The developmental age equivalent of the Mental and Motor Scales raw scores**
   (a) are the most psychometrically sound scores.
   (b) vary by the child's chronological age.
   (c) can be a clear way to report an infant's performance.
   (d) should never be reported.

continued

7. The BRS is completed by the examiner after the administration of the BSID-II. True or False?

8. Examiners who deviate from the administrative procedures on the BSID-II

(a) should use the norms to calculate MDI and PDI scores; deviating from the standard procedures usually has little impact on the infant's scores.

(b) should not report anything beyond general descriptions.

(c) should explain how they deviated from the standard procedures and report developmental ages.

(d) should never deviate from the standardized procedures.

Answers: 1. False; 2. b; 3. True; 4. False; 5. False; 6. c; 7. True; 8. c

Four

HOW TO INTERPRET THE BSID-II

The interpretation of scores from the BSID-II is similar to the process of solving a complex puzzle. Each piece of information contributes to the overall picture, but cannot be understood independently or out of context. The MDI and PDI scores are important, but they do not provide the entire picture. In addition to test scores, accurate interpretation of the BSID-II requires information about the infant's medical and social history, prior test performance, as well as the specific conditions surrounding the testing situation (see Don't Forget 4.1). For example, the interpretation of scores may differ for an infant who is recovering from an illness versus an infant who is healthy or an infant who has been participating in an early intervention program.

Examiners should also remember that testing situations are artificial estimates of infants' abilities, and all tests contain errors. Thus some children will

DON'T FORGET

4.1 Behavior Rating Scale

- BSID-II scores should not be interpreted without considering the BRS, caregiver report, results from other tests, and medical records.
- The BRS aids in the interpretation of the MDI and PDI scores. If the total score and the three factor scores (Orientation/Engagement and Emotional Regulation, or Attention/Arousal) are Within Normal Limits, the examiner can feel relatively confident about the validity of the evaluation. In contrast, if these scores on the BRS are in the Questionable or Non-Optimal range, the examiner should determine whether the maladaptive behavior is temporary (possibly associated with an illness or fatigue) or a relatively stable component of the infant's temperament.

obtain scores outside the normal limits purely by chance. Examiners should not rely solely on scores from the BSID-II but should integrate the scores with other information obtained from the caregiver, medical record, or other tests. If the examiner doubts the validity of the results from the BSID-II, the test (or portions of the test) should be repeated.

MENTAL AND PSYCHOMOTOR DEVELOPMENTAL INDEXES

Interpretation of scores begins with the MDI and PDI because they are the most psychometrically sound components of the BSID-II. The standardization sample's raw scores on the Mental and Motor Scales were converted to index scores, or normalized scores (see Don't Forget 4.2).

The index scores were calculated assuming a normal distribution of scores (bell-shaped curve; see Rapid Reference 4.1). The mean of the MDI and PDI is 100, which is the average score of all infants in the standardization sample. In a normal distribution, the mode, or most common score, and the median, or score at the 50th percentile, are also 100. Thus, within the standardization sample of the BSID-II, the most frequent MDI or PDI score is 100 and half the infants obtained scores above 100 and half obtained scores below 100.

Norms are provided for 38 age categories. For the first 36 months, the norms are calculated in 1-month intervals. Beyond 36 months, norms are calculated in 3-month intervals. For example, the table for the 8-month norms spans 7 months, 16 days, to 8 months, 15 days. The 37- to 39-month norms are for infants between 36 months, 16 days, and 39 months, 15 days.

DON'T FORGET

4.2 BSID-II Index Scores

Norms Tables for the MDI and PDI are based on the standardization sample. Scores range from 50 to 150.

For the MDI and PDI, the mean is 100 and the standard deviation is 15.

Standard Deviation

The standard deviation is a measure of the variability of the scores, that is, how they are distributed around the mean (see Don't Forget 4.2). The scores for the BSID-II have been smoothed to approximate a normal distribution. In a normal distribution most scores (68%) are within 1 standard devia-

≡ Rapid Reference

4.1 Normal Distribution

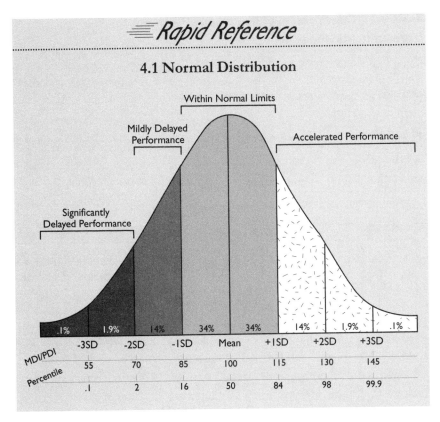

Within Normal Limits

Mildly Delayed Performance

Accelerated Performance

Significantly Delayed Performance

	.1%	1.9%	14%	34%	34%	14%	1.9%	.1%
	-3SD	-2SD	-1SD	Mean	+1SD	+2SD	+3SD	
MDI/PDI	55	70	85	100	115	130	145	
Percentile	.1	2	16	50	84	98	99.9	

tion above or below the mean. The standard deviation for the MDI and PDI is 15. Therefore 68% of the infants in the standardization sample obtained scores between 85 and 115. Scores in this range are considered Within Normal Limits (see Table 4.1, page 68).

In a normal distribution, approximately 16% of the scores are more than 1 standard deviation above the mean, or above 115. Thus approximately 16% of the infants in the standardization sample obtain scores above 115. Infants who achieve MDI or PDI scores that are 115 and above are in the Accelerated Performance classification.

Similarly, approximately 16% of the scores are more than 1 standard deviation below the mean, or below 85. Thus approximately 16% of the infants in the standardization sample obtain scores below 85. Infants who achieve MDI or PDI scores that are between 70 and 84 are in the Mildly Delayed Performance classification.

Table 4.1   Classification of Mental and Psychomotor Developmental Index Scores

In both the BSID and BSID-II, the mean of the mental and motor indices is 100. However, the standard deviation has been revised from 16 for the BSID to 15 for the BSID-II, to be more consistent with other standardized tests.

Score Range	Classification	Expected Percentage
115 and above	Accelerated Performance	16.0
85–114	Within Normal Limits	68.0
70–84	Mildly Delayed Performance	13.5
69 and below	Significantly Delayed Performance	2.5

Note. BSID-II scores range from 50 to 150. From the *Manual for the Bayley Scales of Infant Development: Second Edition.* Copyright © 1993 by The Psychological Corporation. Reproduced by permission. All rights reserved.

Only 2% of the infants in the standardization sample obtained scores that were more than two standard deviations above mean (above 130) and 2% obtained scores that were more than 2 standard deviations below the mean (below 70). Infants with MDI or PDI scores below 70 are in the Significantly Delayed Performance classification (see Table 4.1). Fewer than 0.1% of the infants in the standardization sample obtained scores that were more than 3 standard deviations above or below the mean (below 55 or above 145). Therefore the norms for the MDI and PDI do not extend below 50 or above 150.

Standard Error of Measurement and Confidence Intervals

Examiners should always be aware of the standard error of measurement, which represents the error inherent in any test. The formula for calculating the standard error includes the test's reliability—the likelihood of obtaining the same score if the test were administered twice. When reliability is high, standard error is small and the examiner can be relatively confident that the infant's obtained score is a good estimate of the true score.

The standard error of measurement was calculated for each age of administration for the Mental and Motor Scales. The average standard error of measurement is 5.21 for the Mental Scale and 6.01 for the Motor Scale. There is little variability across age. The standard error of measurement can be used to calculate confidence intervals. In calculating confidence intervals for the BSID-II MDI and PDI scores, the standard error of estimation was used rather than the standard error of measurement to correct for regression to the mean. A confidence interval represents the likelihood that the infant's true score is within a specified range (see Don't Forget 4.3). Thus, according to the published confidence intervals, if a 12-month-old infant obtains an MDI of 72, the examiner can claim with 95% confidence that the infant's true score is between 66 and 84. The use of confidence intervals can be particularly helpful if the examiner thinks the infant would benefit from early intervention services and the infant obtains a score that is slightly beyond the cutoff. The examiner can argue that there is high likelihood that the infant's true score is within the criteria established for early intervention.

> **DON'T FORGET**
> ....
> **4.3 Confidence Intervals**
>
> All test scores include measurement error. The confidence interval defines the range in which the infant's true score is likely to fall. The BSID-II provides intervals at two levels of confidence: 90% and 95%. These intervals are provided in the Norms Tables. The use of confidence intervals can be helpful in qualifying an infant for intervention services.

Comparisons Between the BSID-II and BSID

The scores on the BSID have drifted upward such that the mean MDI was approximately 112 and the mean PDI was approximately 111 (Campbell et al., 1986). Within a subset of the standardization sample who were administered both the BSID and the BSID-II, the average BSID MDI was 111.6 and the average PDI was 110.5. Therefore infants who have been tested using the BSID are likely to have lower scores when they are tested using the BSID-II (see Table 4.3). Similarly, the BSID-II MDI and PDI scores are often lower than scores from other developmental assessments that were either based on the BSID or developed in the past without renorming. This discrepancy in scores can cause confusion among colleagues and caregivers (see Table 4.3). Examiners can often avoid confusion by explaining the discrepancy in scores

Table 4.2   Relation of MDI and PDI Scores to Percentile Ranks

MDI or PDI	Percentile (based on theoretical normal distribution)	Number of Standard Deviations From the Mean
145	99.9	+3
140	99.6	+2.66
135	99	+2.33
130	98	+2
125	95	+1.66
120	91	+1.33
115	84	+1
110	75	+0.66
105	63	+0.33
100	50	0 (mean)
95	37	−0.33
90	25	−0.66
85	16	−1
80	9	−1.33
75	5	−1.66
70	2	−2
65	1	−2.33
60	0.4	−2.66
55	0.1	−3
50 and below	<0.1	<−3.33

Note. It is often helpful to use percentiles when interpreting scores to caregivers. From the *Manual for the Bayley Scales Infant Development: Second Edition.* Copyright © 1993 by The Psychological Corporation. Reproduced by permission. All rights reserved.

Table 4.3   Comparison of MDI and PDI Scores on the BSID and BSID-II

BSID MDI/PDI Score	BSID-II MDI Score	BSID-II PDI Score
50		
55	50–56	
60	50–60	
65	55–64	50–54
70	59–68	50–60
75	64–72	55–65
80	69–76	61–71
85	74–80	68–76
90	78–84	75–82
95	88–92	82–87
100	92–96	88–93
105	92–96	94–99
110	97–100	101–105
115	101–105	107–111
120	105–109	113–118
125	109–114	119–124
130	113–118	124–131
135	117–123	130–138
140	121–128	135–144
145		141–150
150		146–150

Note. From the *Manual for the Bayley Scales Infant Development: Second Edition.* Copyright © 1993 by The Psychological Corporation. Reproduced by permission. All rights reserved.

from the beginning. Because the BSID-II is a better normed test than most other developmental assessments, the examiner should have confidence in the norms.

MDI and PDI Scores Below 50

The norms from the standardization sample do not go below 50 for the MDI or PDI. Since the standardization sample was designed to be representative of infants in the United States, and fewer than 0.1% of the infants in the population would be expected to obtain a score less than 50, there were very few infants in the standardization sample with an MDI or PDI score below 50. However, the BSID-II is often used with infants who are developmentally delayed. Examiners often need more discrimination for an infant's level of functioning below 50. One option is to convert the raw scores into developmental age scores, as shown in Table B.2 (p. 325) of the BSID-II manual and reproduced in Table 4.4. For example an infant of 24 months

Table 4.4   Conversion of Raw Scores on the Mental and Motor Scales Into Developmental Ages

Mental Scale Raw Score	Estimated Developmental Age (in months)	Motor Scale Raw Score
0–13	<1	0–10
14–21	1	11–14
22–31	2	15–21
32–40	3	22–27
41–51	4	28–32
52–60	5	33–37
61–65	6	38–43
66–70	7	44–50
71–74	8	51–55
75–77	9	56
78–80	10	57–60
81–86	11	61–63
87–90	12	64–66

Table 4.4 continued

Mental Scale Raw Score	Estimated Developmental Age (in months)	Motor Scale Raw Score
91–93	13	67
94–97	14	68–69
98–101	15	70–71
102–106	16	72–73
107–111	17	74–75
112–115	18	76
116–119	19	77
120–122	20	78
123–125	21	79–80
126–128	22	81–82
129–131	23	83
132–134	24	84–85
135–137	25	86–87
138–140	26	88–89
141–143	27	90–91
	28	92
144–145	29	93
146–147	30	94
148	31	95
149–150	32	96
151	33	97
152	34	98
153–154	35	99
155–157	36	100
158–162	37–39	101–103
163–165	40–42	104–105
166–178	>42	106–111

who obtains a raw score between 1 and 107 on the Mental Scale would receive an MDI of below 50. A raw score of 107 on the Mental Scale is equivalent to a developmental age of 17 months, a raw score of 78 is equivalent to a developmental age score of 10 months, and a raw score of 30 is equivalent to a developmental age score of 2 months. By using developmental ages, the examiner can provide an estimate of the infant's mental or motor skills.

Another alternative is to use extrapolated norms for the BSID-II provided by Robinson and Mervis (1996). Using statistical techniques rather than empirical data, they have provided estimated raw scores for MDI and PDI scores from 30 to 50 (see Table 4.5). These scores can be used as a guide in describing an infant's performance and in tracking an infant's developmental progress, but the examiner must remember that the scores are estimates and not based on actual data. For example, if an infant who was enrolled into an early intervention program at age 9 months with an MDI of 30 was retested 12 months later and found to have an MDI of 45, the interpretation would be that the infant had made excellent progress. In contrast, if the infant's score was recorded as less than 50 at enrollment and less than 50 after 12 months of intervention, it would be difficult to determine the effects of intervention. Examiners who rely on extrapolated scores must always add a caveat to their reports, noting that the scores were estimated. In addition, examiners who work with severely delayed infants who receive scores below 50 must remember that the development of severely delayed infants is often uneven, particularly if they are experiencing disabling conditions and/or chronic medical problems, such as seizure disorders (see Don't Forget 4.4).

Table 4.5   Extrapolated Raw Scores for the MDI and PDI

Extrapolated Raw Scores for the MDI

	Age in Months															
MDI	2	3	4	5	6	8	10	12	15	18	21	24	27	30	36	42
50	3			38	47	55		74			99	108	117		130	140
49		8	19	30				65	73	87				122		
48	2			37	46						98	107	116		129	139
47		7	18	29			54	64	72	86				121		
46	1			36	45						97	106	115		128	138
45		6	17	28			53	63	71	85				120		
44				35	44						96	105	114		127	137
43		5	16	27			52	62	70	84				119		
42				34	43						95	104	113		126	136
41		4	15	26			51	61	69	83				118		
40				33	42						94	103	112		125	135
39		3	14	25			50	60	68	82				117		
38				32	41						93	102	111		124	134
37		2	13	24			49		67	81				116		
36				31	40			59			92	101	110		123	133
35		1	12	23			48		66	80				115		
34				30	39			58			91	100	109		122	132
33			11	22			47		65	79				114		
32				29	38			57			90	99	108		121	131
31			10	21					64	78				113		
30				28	37		46	56			89	98	107		120	130

continued

Table 4.5 continued

Extrapolated Raw Scores for the PDI

PDI									Age in Months							
	2	3	4	5	6	8	10	12	15	18	21	24	27	30	36	42
50																
49	8			23				52	57		66	71	77		84	
48			17													92
47		11				35	41			62				80		
46	7			22				51							83	
45			16						56		65	70	76			
44		10				34	40									91
43	6			21						61				79	82	
42		9	15					50			64	69				
41						33	39		55				75			90
40	5			20											81	
39			14							60				78		
38		8				32	38	49				68				
37	4			19					54		63		74		80	
36			13													89
35		7				31	37			59				77		
34	3			18				48				67			79	
33		6	12				36		53		62		73			
32						30										88
31	2			17						58				76	78	
30		5	11			29	35	47				66				

Note. The BSID-II standardization sample represents national norms. The standardization sample excluded infants with severe delays or medical conditions that placed the infants at risk for developmental PDI delays. Therefore the range of scores is truncated and does not include children with severe delays. Scores below 50 should be interpreted with care because the scores are extrapolated and because development in children with severe delays is often uneven. To interpret scores below 50, convert raw scores to developmental age and use extrapolated norms (Robinson & Mervis, 1996). From "Extrapolated raw scores for the second edition of the Bayley Scales of Infant Development," by B. F. Robinson and C. B. Mervis, 1996, *American Journal on Mental Retardation, 100,* pp. 666–670. Copyright © 1996 by the American Association on Mental Retardation. Reproduced with permission. All rights reserved.

Differences in MDI and PDI Scores

Examiners should always compare the infant's performance on the Mental and Motor Scales. Under normal circumstances, an infant's performance is comparable on the Mental and Motor Scales. Statistically, an average difference in MDI and PDI scores of 15.5 points is significant at the .05 level of significance (see Table 5.8 in the BSID-II manual). At the same time, 30% of the infants in the standardization sample had an MDI score that was at least 15 points higher than their PDI score and 34% of the infants had a PDI score that was at least 15 points higher than their MDI score (see Table 4.6). Thus statistically significant differences in scores are not necessarily rare events. However, examiners should regard significant differences in scores as a possible concern that should be evaluated carefully.

The MDI is often given more importance than the PDI, in what has been referred to as cognitive referencing (Cole & Harris, 1992). That is, regardless of an infant's performance on the Motor Scale, performance on the MDI is often conceptualized as a measure of the infant's abilities, as though the

Table 4.6   Cumulative Percentage of MDI-PDI Discrepancies in the Standardization Sample

Discrepancy Points	Percentage With MDI > PDI	Percentage With PDI > MDI
50	0.8	0.7
45	1.2	1.0
40	2.4	2.6
35	4.8	4.6
30	8.3	7.9
25	12.9	13.5
20	20.6	22.0
15	30.2	34.4
10	48.8	50.2
5	74.4	70.1
0	100	100

Motor Scale represents merely a maturational unfolding. However, mental and motor skills are interdependent, especially during the first months of life as infants use their emerging motor skills to explore their surroundings. Unfortunately, there have been few studies that have investigated the clinical significance of MDI-PDI differences. In a notable exception, MDI-PDI differences were investigated in a recent follow-up evaluation of infants who were identified as high risk based on perinatal factors (e.g., low birth weight, low Apgar scores, etc.) (Aylward, Verhulst, Bell, & Gyurke, 1995). The MDI-PDI differences were relatively small (statistically insignificant) and not influenced by socioeconomic status or social support. Among infants with higher levels of cognitive functioning, MDI scores were higher than PDI scores, but among infants with low levels of cognitive functioning, PDI scores were higher than MDI scores. More research is needed to determine the clinical implications of MDI-PDI differences.

If there is a significant MDI-PDI discrepancy, the examiner should review the infant's pattern of performance, behavior during performance, medical record, and psychosocial history to determine if there is an explanation for the discrepancy. There are at least four possible explanations for MDI-PDI differences. First, if an infant's PDI is lower than the MDI and the motor items were administered at the end of the session, as they usually are, the infant may have been tired and no longer compliant or cooperative. Second, if the BSID-II was administered in a language that is not familiar to the infant, or if the infant has a hearing impairment, it would not be surprising for the infant's MDI, which relies on verbal instruction, to be lower than the PDI, which relies heavily on imitation. Third, an infant who is experiencing failure to thrive, muscle wastage, or a neuromuscular problem may have depressed PDI scores, but not necessarily depressed MDI scores. Finally, differences in scores may also point to the possibility of specific language or learning deficits. For example, an infant with a language delay may have depressed MDI scores but not necessarily depressed PDI scores. In this case, the examiner should look at the pattern of the infant's scores on the items from Mental Scale to determine how well the infant's abilities are balanced among the specific mental processes in that item set. In summary, examiners should measure the discrepancy between MDI and PDI scores. If the discrepancy is statistically significant and relatively uncommon, examiners should look for possible explanations.

PATTERN OF SCORES AT THE ITEM LEVEL

The items on the Mental and Motor Scales are arranged in order of difficulty. Therefore most infants receive credit for items at the beginning of the item set (items with the lowest numbers). As the items become more difficult (and the numbers get higher), infants frequently demonstrate a pattern of credited items mixed with "no-credit" items. Finally, the infant reaches a ceiling and stops receiving credit, so the last items (those with the highest numbers) are no-credit items. The examiner should look at the infant's pattern of responses and raise questions if the infant deviates from the expected pattern. For example, an infant who does not receive credit for relatively easy items but does receive credit for more difficult items may have a specific disability. The examiner should look at the no-credit items to determine if they tap a specific area of functioning (e.g., language, perceptual-motor). A language-delayed infant may receive no credit for all the language items but receive credit for other items at the same relative difficulty that do not tap language skills. Many times an infant with a language delay has an aversion to the Stimulus Booklet and refuses to look at it.

Discrepancies in the pattern of scores may also be related to behavioral issues. For example, an infant with limited stamina may tire easily and have difficulty completing the final items administered, regardless of their level of difficulty. The examiner should be aware of changes in the infant's level of attention and cooperation that might explain discrepancies in scores.

DEVELOPMENTAL DELAY VERSUS DEVELOPMENTAL DISABILITY

Infants who experience developmental delays are following an expected developmental course, but at a slower rate. For example, many premature infants experience early developmental delays but catch up with no long-term consequences.

In contrast, infants with developmental disabilities have atypical development and are not following an expected course. For example, a child with cerebral palsy is developmentally disabled because the movement patterns associated with cerebral palsy do not occur among normally developing infants. It may be easier to recognize problems among infants with developmental disabilities than those with developmental delays because the atypical patterns are more obvious than developmental delay. The BRS is particularly helpful in determining if a child has a disability because it enables the examiner to describe the quality of an infant's motor skills. Thus a hypertonic child would have a Motor Quality score that indicated an abnormal pattern of motor quality. Severity of disability can be further interpreted by looking at the Motor Quality in relation to the PDI to gauge the impact of muscle tone and movement or motor development. The more abnormal the Motor Quality, the greater the impact it is likely to have on the PDI.

PREDICTABILITY

The predictability of scores from infant assessments has attracted a great deal of attention during the past several decades. From early longitudinal studies with young children, Bayley concluded that there is little predictability from early mental scores to later IQ scores or to school functioning (Bayley, 1933). The lack of predictability is not surprising because the skills measured in infant assessments, which often reflect early sensorimotor development, are very different from the language, perceptual, and performance-based information processing skills that constitute intelligence at later ages. In addition, some theorists have conceptualized mental development during the first 18 to 24 months of life as a highly canalized process that is guided by species-specific paths (McCall, 1981). Based on this theory, strong self-righting processes protect young infants from all but the most devastating environmental influences. However, after the first 18 to 24 months, development is less canalized, self-righting processes are less effective, and individual differences stabilize (Kopp & McCall, 1982). Without the protection of the self-righting processes, the influence of genetics and environment becomes more apparent. Several longitudinal studies with infants and young children from low-income families have provided compelling evidence for the normalcy of developmental scores in the first year or two of life, followed by a significant decline in scores through the preschool years (Burchinal, Campbell, Bryant, Wasik, & Ramey, 1997; Luster & McAdoo, 1996; Ramey & Campbell, 1991; Schweinhart & Weikart, 1989; Werner, Bierman, & French, 1971; Werner & Smith, 1982). Prior to age 2 years, poverty does not seem to have a major impact on children's development; however, after 2 years of age, poverty has a negative influence on the developmental test scores of children in

low-income families. There are multiple pathways whereby poverty may
undermine children's development,
including compromised health and
nutrition, limited appropriate stimulation in the home, less sensitive
parent-child interactions, parental
mental health problems, and lack of
stimulating neighborhood opportunities (Brooks-Gunn & Duncan,
1997). Thus developmental assessments administered after age 2 are

> # CAUTION
> ## 4.1 Predictability of Infant Test Scores
> The predictability of infant test scores to later IQ or academic functioning is low. Predictability is often better when specific cognitive processes are considered or among infants who exhibit substantial developmental delays.

more likely to be predictive of later intelligence and academic performance
than assessments administered in the first 24 months of life (see Caution 4.1).

Researchers and clinicians agree that predictability is best at the lower levels of functioning, presumably because infants with low cognitive scores have
significant organic problems or environmental insults that are so severe that
they disrupt the self-righting process (Aylward & Kenny, 1979; Siegel, 1981,
1982). Among preterm infants, predictability to preschool test scores improves
when Bayley scores are combined with measures of risk (e.g., birth weight)
and socioeconomic status, demonstrating the multiple factors that influence
children's cognitive abilities (Siegel, 1982).

Researchers who have moved away from global assessments of infant
development, such as the BSID-II, and who have focused on specific aspects
of information processing, have found consistencies between specific cognitive abilities measured during infancy and later measures of IQ (DiLalla et al.,
1990; Fagan et al., 1986; Rose & Feldman, 1995). Examiners should be aware
of this line of research, but most of the measures of infant abilities used by
researchers are experimental and have not undergone the level of psychometric scrutiny that has been applied to the BSID-II. Thus there is much to learn
about the determinants of childhood and adult functioning and the predictability of measures of information processing from infancy.

Similarly, investigators have combined specific items from the Bayley into
subtests. For example, Siegel, Cooper, Fitzhardinge, and Ash (1995) formed
subtests of expressive and receptive language items and found these subtests
to be useful in identifying children with language delays. However, caution is

warranted because the BSID-II wasn't developed to produce separate, reliable, and valid subtest scores across the ages. Also, while expressive and receptive language may be clearly defined content areas, the specific content area that other items tap would require more validation.

Despite questions regarding predictability, the BSID-II is widely used to measure infant development so that infants whose development is delayed can receive intervention as early as possible.

FACET SCORES

The facet scores were developed to provide information about the infant's performance in four areas of development: Cognitive, Language, Motor, and Social. Items were classified into the four areas on the consensus ratings of nine reviewers, verified by item-to-total correlations. The mental and motor items were combined and the relative difficulty of each item was determined using Rasch difficulty estimates. Item difficulty was regressed on age to assign items to developmental ages within each facet. Although most of the items follow the ordinal sequence that appears within the Mental and Motor Scales, at times the sequence differs with "easier" items placed at slightly older ages than "more difficult" items (e.g., in the Cognitive facet, 118 is a 17-month item, and 112 is a 19-month item). See the more detailed discussion in Chapter 3.

Although the facet scores can be helpful in describing an infant's performance in specific areas, they must be used with caution because there is not equal representation of items across the ages within facets (see Caution 4.2). The Cognitive facet contains the most items and the items span the age range from 1 to 42 months. In contrast, the Social facet contains the fewest number of items and is not a useful description of social behavior beyond the first 4 months.

Most of the items in the Language facet pertain to language below 23 months of age. One use of

> ## CAUTION
> ....
> ### 4.2 Facets
>
> The facets may be helpful in describing an infant's performance in four specific areas of development: Motor, Language, Cognitive, or Social. However, some of the facets contain very few items. For example, the Social facet is only useful within the first few months of life.

the facet scores is to identify language delay. By plotting an infant's facet scores, the examiner can compare language and cognitive performance. For example, an infant whose Language score is at a 12-month level and whose Cognitive score is at a 17-month level may have a language delay and should be referred for language and audiology evaluations.

The facets provide a general description of an infant's functioning within each of the four constructs, but they do not yield precise scores. Examiners who need precise scores in each area should look to other developmental assessments (e.g., Battelle Developmental Inventory; Newborg et al., 1984).

BEHAVIOR RATING SCALE

The BRS is a critical component of interpretation because it captures aspects of the infant's approach to structured tasks. Because the factor structure for the BRS differs slightly across ages, the BRS is divided into three age groupings: 0 to 5 months, 6 to 12 months, and 13 to 42 months (see Rapid Reference 4.2). Motor quality is assessed at all ages and is a welcome addition to the Bayley Scales because it captures the quality of the infant's movements through items such as hypertonicity, hypotonicity, tremulousness, motor control, and frenetic movements. Thus the Motor Quality Factor on the BRS enables the examiner to describe the quality of the infant's motor skills, regardless of his or her ability to complete the items on the Motor Scale. For example, hypotonicity may interfere with an infant's ability to sit or crawl. With the Motor Quality factor, the examiner can comment directly on hypotonicity.

Attention/Arousal is a factor in the 1- to 5-month-old group. It refers to the infant's predominant state, arousal, affect, interest in test materials, orien-

≡ Rapid Reference

4.2 BRS Factors

Age Group:	1–5 months	6–12, 13–42 months
	Attention/Arousal	Orientation/Engagement
	Motor Quality	Emotional Regulation
		Motor Quality

tation to the examiner, and sensitivity to the materials. When an infant has a low score on the Attention/Arousal factor, the examiner should consider the representativeness of the infant's test behavior. For example, infants who are tired, ill, or under stress may appear to be irritable and disinterested, with a short attention span. Low Attention/Arousal scores may also signify neurological immaturity. For example, a premature infant may lack the stamina to maintain arousal throughout the test session.

Two other factors in the 6- to 12-month and the 13- to 42-month groupings are Orientation/Engagement, and Emotional Regulation. Orientation/Engagement is similar to Attention/Arousal in that it includes items that address the infant's predominant state, level of arousal, positive affect, energy, initiative, enthusiasm, and persistence. Motor Quality is similar to Motor Quality in the 1- to 5-month group. Emotional Regulation includes items on the infant's orientation to the examiner, sensitivity to test materials, frustration, cooperation, attention, and adaptability to changes in test materials.

Within each factor, at each age, the raw scores are converted into percentiles. Infants who obtain a score between the 1st and 10th percentile are classified as displaying behavior that is Non-Optimal, children who score between the 11th and 25th percentile are classified as having Questionable behavior, and children with a score at or above the 26th percentile are classified as having behavior that is Within Normal Limits (see Table 4.7).

In the standardization sample, when the BRS scores were compared with the MDI and PDI scores, the correlations were low to moderate, ranging from .13 to .46, depending upon age group and factor. Although the BRS is related to MDI and PDI performance, correlations at this level suggest that the BRS measures variance that is unique from that of the MDI and PDI. A classification system was developed to examine the likelihood that children who obtained MDI and PDI scores greater than or equal to 70 would also obtain BRS scores above the 10th percentile (Within Normal Limits and Questionable) and who obtained MDI and PDI scores lower than 70 would obtain BRS scores at the 10th percentile or less (Non-Optimal). Correct classification was only moderate. Among clinical samples (infants with Down syndrome, developmental delay, and autistic disorders) there was a higher percentage of infants with BRS scores in the Non-Optimal range, with 100% of the infants with Autistic Disorders falling in the Non-Optimal range.

The BRS is useful in estimating the validity of the MDI and PDI. For example, if an infant's BRS scores for Orientation/Engagement and Emotional

Table 4.7   Classification of BRS Percentiles

Percentile Range	Classification	Percentage of Standardized Population
1–10	Non-Optimal	10
11–25	Questionable	15
26–99	Within Normal Limits	75

Regulation are Within Normal Limits, then the examiner may feel more confident that the infant's performance on the Mental and Motor Scales is an accurate representation of his or her skills. In contrast, if the infant is not attentive or not cooperative and obtains BRS scores in the Questionable or Non-Optimal range, the examiner should question whether the infant's behavior interfered with her or his performance on the Mental and Motor Scales. In this case, it is very helpful to review the caregiver's assessment of the infant's behavior. If the caregiver reports that the infant's behavior was atypical, then the examiner should look for an alternative explanation for the infant's behavior and perhaps schedule the infant for a reevaluation. On the other hand, if the caregiver reports that such behavior is typical, then the examiner must decide whether to refer the infant for behavior management and try to interpret the MDI and PDI scores in light of the infant's behavior problems.

Studies of the Infant Behavior Record, the predecessor to the BRS, revealed continuity in the pattern of scores from the Infant Behavior Record through the first 2 years of life (Matheny, 1983). Factor analyses of the scales from the Infant Behavior Record were performed on a sample of 300 to 400 infant twins tested through the first 2 years of life (Matheny, 1981). Major factors were Task Orientation, Affect-Extraversion, Activity, Auditory-Visual Awareness, and Motor Coordination. These characteristics have been incorporated into the BRS.

INTERPRETING SCORES TO CAREGIVERS AND COLLEAGUES

The results from the BSID-II can be interpreted to caregivers and colleagues using index scores, percentiles, and developmental ages. Index scores (MDI and PDI) are frequently used when communicating with colleagues. They are the most psychometrically sound of the choices and can be used to compare an infant's progress over time or to compare the performance of two infants of different ages. However, index scores are sometimes difficult for caregivers to understand. A second option when interpreting scores to caregivers or to colleagues is to use percentiles. Since many people are more familiar with percentiles than with index scores, percentiles are a useful way to represent an infant's performance relative to all the infants in the standardization sample. As shown in Table 4.2, an infant who obtains an MDI of 100 is at the 50th percentile. In other words, 50% of the infants in the standardization sample obtained higher scores and 50% obtained lower scores. Similarly, an infant who obtains an MDI of 70 is at the 2nd percentile, meaning that 98% of the infants in the standardization sample obtained higher scores and 2% obtained lower scores. Reporting percentiles is often a less precise representation than index scores because Table 7.1 (p. 228) in the BSID-II manual does not contain all index scores. When a score does not appear in Table 7.1, the examiner must report a percentile range (e.g., an MDI or PDI or 92 is between the 25th and 37th percentiles). A third option is to convert the raw scores into developmental age equivalents, as shown in Table B.2 (p. 325) of the BSID-II manual and reproduced in Table 4.4. Developmental age can be a useful concept, but as noted in Chapter 3, there are three potential drawbacks. First, examiners must clarify that the developmental age refers only to those abilities assessed with the BSID-II and not necessarily to other aspects of the infant's development, such as physical growth, self-help skills, or social maturity. Second, developmental age may be confusing when an infant has a developmental profile that is atypical, rather than merely delayed. Finally, developmental age may not represent an infant's skills accurately when the infant has uneven development. This problem occurs more frequently on the Mental Scale than the Motor Scale because the Mental Scale represents an eclectic combination of cognitive skills, including language skills.

It is never easy to tell caregivers that their infant is developmentally delayed or disabled, even when the caregiver suspects that there is a problem. It is often useful to begin by asking caregivers about their thoughts regarding their child's development. The examiner can confirm suspicions or gently lead caregivers toward recognizing that their infant's skills are not as advanced "as we wish they were." It is also helpful to focus caregivers on the future by explaining that infancy is a period of rapid change and it is important to evaluate their infant's ability to acquire skills over the next 6 or 12 months to get a better picture of the infant's developmental potential. Examiners should not minimize the infant's developmental delays or tell caregivers that the infant may "outgrow" the problem because this would mislead families and because families who do not acknowledge a problem may be less inclined to take advantage of early intervention programs. Furthermore, many infants do not outgrow problems that are identified in infancy, particularly when their MDI or PDI scores are below 70 and hence have a Significantly Delayed Performance classification.

Caregivers should have a clear understanding about their infant's developmental status, so their expectations and developmental stimulation are appropriate for the infant's needs. Helping caregivers recognize their infant's strengths and focusing on anticipatory guidance can be beneficial to infants. Although caregivers should be educated about their infant's medical diagnosis, noncategorical terms, such as developmental delay, are usually used during infancy. Diagnostic classifications, such as mental retardation, are usually not given during the first several years of life before children's developmental profile has stabilized.

Examiners should avoid making a long-term prognosis on the infant's developmental skills. It is often helpful to inform caregivers about early intervention and family support programs. Early intervention programs offer therapy and classes for children that often include parents.

🖋 TEST YOURSELF 🖋

1. **Most infants obtain MDI scores above 100.** True or False?
2. **A score of 125 on the MDI is classified as Accelerated Performance.** True or False?
3. **An infant who obtains an MDI of 90 is at the 90th percentile.** True or False?
4. **Infants who obtain an MDI or PDI below 50**
   (a) usually have hearing impairments.
   (b) are significantly delayed.
   (c) rarely have behavior problems.
   (d) represent about 20% of the population.

continued

5. **Scores from the BSID-II are generally about 10 points higher than scores from other developmental assessments.** True or False?

6. **It is relatively common to have a discrepancy of about 5 points between MDI and PDI scores.** True or False?

7. **Infant assessments, such as the BSID-II**

   (a) are excellent predictors of school-age IQ.

   (b) are only predictive if infants speak English.

   (c) become more predictive for infants over 2 years of age.

   (d) should not be given to children from low-income families.

8. **Facet scores yield precise scores in Motor, Cognitive, Language, and Social.** True or False?

9. **The BRS is extremely helpful in interpreting MDI and PDI scores.** True or False?

Answers: 1. False; 2. True; 3. False; 4. b; 5. False; 6. True; 7. c; 8. False; 9. True

Five

There were seven major goals set forth for the revision of the BSID. These goals were based on critiques of the BSID and contemporary standards of psychological assessments. The seven goals were to update the norms, extend the age range down to 1 month and up to 42 months, improve content coverage, update materials, improve the psychometric quality and clinical utility, while preserving the basic structure of the test. This chapter reviews the strengths and weaknesses of the BSID-II in relation to most of these goals (see Rapid Reference 5.1). The information is based largely on feedback from examiners who have contacted the Psychological Corporation, issues raised in workshops and in the literature, and the experience of the authors and colleagues.

NORMATIVE DATA

The BSID-II, published in 1993, was a welcome revision to infant examiners. Although the BSID was widely used and respected, examiners were well aware that the norms were no longer accurate (Campbell et al., 1986). The provision of updated norms is one of the primary strengths of the BSID-II. The standardization sample was chosen to reflect the 1988 U.S. census. Infants were included in the standardization sample in accordance with census figures on race, parental education, and region. For example, 14.8% of the infants in the sample were African American and 11.6% were Hispanic, comparable to the percentages of African Americans and Hispanics in the 1988 census. The sample includes an equal number of boys and girls by age.

One weakness of the BSID-II with respect to the norms is that it does not provide data on infants whose parents do not speak English. Given the increasing number of Spanish speakers in the United States, there is a clear need to

≡ Rapid Reference

5.1 Strengths and Weaknesses in the Standardization of BSID-II

Strengths

- Scale was standardized using 1988 U.S. census figures for parental race, education, region, and infant's gender.
- Clinical samples have been included to demonstrate validity of BSID-II.
- The age of BSID-II extends from 1 to 42 months.
- There is excellent construct validity with an expected pattern of correlations between BSID-II Scales and McCarthy Scales of Children's Abilities, Wechsler Preschool and Primary Scales of Intelligence–Revised, Differential Ability Scales, and Pre-School Language Scale–3.
- Tables are provided for converting Mental and Motor Scale raw scores to index scores and developmental age equivalents.
- There is a strong emphasis on adhering to procedures used during standardization.
- Strong psychometric properties exist for the MDI and PDI.
- Tables are provided to compare BSID scores and BSID-II scores.

Weaknesses

- There are no guidelines for using the BSID-II among infants from non-English-speaking families and no guidelines for standardizing in other populations.
- Presentation of clinical samples is extremely limited (e.g., small sample sizes, heterogeneous groups).
- There is less coverage of items from 30 to 42 months.
- There is no provision for non-English-speaking infants.
- Index scores do not extend below 50.
- There are minimal guidelines on using BSID-II to evaluate infants with disabilities.
- There is no inclusion of infants with disabilities in development of BSID-II, beyond the infants with special needs included in the clinical validation studies.
- There is no information on predictive validity.

have a Spanish version of the BSID-II. As with the BSID, examiners who wish to use the BSID-II in other settings (e.g., non-English-speaking families or other countries) will have to explore the cultural adaptations that are necessary, along with the psychometric properties of the test in other cultures. The Psychological Corporation does not provide guidelines for adaptation of the BSID-II for use in other languages or with infants from other cultures.

CONTENT COVERAGE

The BSID-II was designed to increase the number of items that assess problem solving, language, and social development. In addition, other areas of development that emerged from the burgeoning research on infant development, prediction, and disruptions to development were included in the BSID-II. These areas are Infant Recognition Memory and Habituation of Attention, Visual Preference/Visual Acuity, Concepts of Numbers and Counting; Quality of Movement; Sensory Integration; and Perceptual-Motor Integration. These new items provide a more comprehensive evaluation of infant development that is useful when describing an infant's strengths and weaknesses. One drawback is that the coverage of these areas is limited and there are not separate scores by area. Inclusion of the new items enables the BSID-II to serve as a neurodevelopmental screener, while providing a comprehensive global assessment of infant functioning.

A weakness of the BSID-II is that it does not provide information about the infant's skills in the five areas of development identified by IDEA 97 (Cognitive, Physical, Communication, Social-Emotional, and Adaptive). The facets can be used to represent an infant's performance in four areas of development (Cognitive, Language, Social, and Motor) and can be useful in differentiating skills among young infants. However, the coverage of items over the age range of the test is uneven, particularly for the Social and Language development (e.g., only three items beyond the 4-month level on the Social facet). The BRS provides information on social functioning in a structured context, but it was not designed to meet the broader definition of social-emotional development more commonly used to determine service eligibility. Examiners often supplement the BSID-II with assessments of adaptive functioning, such as the Vineland Adaptive Behavior Scales (Sparrow, Bulla, & Cicchetti, 1984) or the Scales of Independent Behavior (Bruininks, Woodcock, Weatherman, & Hill, 1984). For assessments of language, examiners often use the Early Language Milestones Scale (Coplan, 1987), the Receptive-Emergent Language Scale (Bzoch & League, 1970), or the Preschool Language Scale–3 (Zimmerman, Steiner, & Pond, 1992).

PSYCHOMETRIC PROPERTIES

The BSID-II manual includes information on the psychometric properties of the BSID-II, including tables to compare scores obtained on the BSID-II with those obtained on the BSID and tables for converting Mental and Motor Scale raw scores to MDI and PDI scores and to developmental age. These tables are easy to use and facilitate interpretation of the BSID-II.

The BSID-II manual also provides data on the construct validity of the BSID-II. Correlations between scores obtained by infants who completed both the BSID-II and other tests of early childhood development are presented in the manual. Correlations are provided with the McCarthy Scales of Children's Abilities, Wechsler Preschool and Primary Scales of Intelligence–Revised, Differential Ability Scales, and Pre-School Language Scale–3. The pattern of correlations across constructs is consistent with expectations of convergent and divergent validity: The MDI is moderately correlated to many different constructs of cognitive ability, particularly to other measures of verbal ability; in contrast, the PDI has low correlations with subtests that assess memory or quantitative abilities, and is moderately correlated with other motor scales (i.e., on the McCarthy). Correlations between the BSID and BSID-II are also consistent with expectations. There are moderate correlations between the two versions of the test (Motor Scales .62, Mental Scales .63), suggesting that while the two versions are clearly related, the BSID-II assesses somewhat different abilities.

ITEM SETS AND THE PREMISE OF ORDINAL SEQUENCES OF DEVELOPMENT

The introduction of age-specific item sets is a major conceptual change in the administration of the BSID-II and has been a primary source of discussion in the literature (Gauthier, Bauer, Messinger, & Closius, 1999; Matula et al., 1997; Ross & Lawson, 1997; Washington et al., 1998). Item sets were designed to reduce the number of items necessary to obtain a valid estimation of an infant's skills. Their use is based on the premise that infant development occurs in an ordinal sequence across multiple areas. That premise underlies the arrangement of items on the Bayley Scales and the criteria for establishing basal and ceiling.

The BSID-II incorporates the establishment of basal and ceiling within item sets. Once the infant achieves a basal, items from previous item sets are not administered because it is assumed that infants are able to perform items below the basal item set. Similarly, once the infant achieves a ceiling, items from subsequent item sets are not administered because it is assumed that the infant is unable to perform item sets above the ceiling item set. Although this assumption may be valid for infants with normal development, such as those in the standardization sample of the BSID-II, it is not necessarily valid for infants with delayed or atypical development. Concerns regarding the use of item sets are particularly strong when applied to the Mental Scale because cognitive development is a complex, higher-order function that comprises multiple areas. The infant who has uneven development, in which one area is delayed or accelerated relative to other areas provides an excellent example. An infant with delayed language development may obtain a basal on nonlanguage items and achieve an MDI that does not reflect the language delay. In contrast, an infant with precocious language development may reach the ceiling on nonlanguage items and achieve an MDI that does not reflect the language acceleration.

Although most concerns and criticisms about the use of item sets have centered on their use with premature infants and infants with delayed or atypical development (Ross & Lawson, 1997; Washington et al., 1998), questions have also been raised about the use of item sets with normally developing infants (Gauthier et al., 1999). Gauthier and colleagues evaluated 78 12-month-old infants using the 11-month, 12-month, and 13-month item sets and reported that 94% of the infants met basal and ceiling criteria in all three item sets. Index scores generated from the 11-month item set were lower than scores generated from the 12-month item set, which were in turn lower than scores from the 13-month item set. Thus decisions regarding the starting item set can have significant implications on the infant's score.

In reference to premature infants, the publishers of the BSID-II provide instructions for adjusting the infant's age by subtracting the number of months and days the infant was born early from the chronological age (e.g., an infant born at 35 weeks [1 month and 5 days early] and tested at a chronological age of 14 months, 4 days, would have an adjusted age of 12 months, 29 days). In deciding whether to apply the adjustment to premature infants, the examiner determines the starting item set and the Norms Table to be used. The examiner must remember that if adjusted age is used to determine the beginning item set, that age must be used for selecting the Norms Table. Under ideal conditions, if the infant's development were proceeding in an ordinal fashion, across all areas of development the examiner would reach the same *raw score* regardless of whether testing began with the age-adjusted item set or the chronological-age item set. If the item set were too high, the examiner would drop to a lower item set to establish basal, and if the item set were too low, the examiner would advance to a higher item set to establish ceiling. However, Washington and colleagues (1998) have shown that premature infants with delayed or atypical development are sometimes able to establish basal and ceiling in multiple item sets, demonstrating that their development is not consistent with the principles of ordinality. If the assumptions underlying the use of item sets (i.e., ordinal sequence of development across multiple areas of development) are not met, the use of item sets with infants who are premature or with delayed or atypical development is called into question.

Age adjustment for premature infants should yield a higher index score than using the chronological age because the examiner is subtracting the time the infant should have been in utero. Unfortunately there has been a great deal of confusion regarding age adjustment (Ross & Lawson, 1997). As a reminder, examiners who choose to adjust for prematurity should calculate the adjusted age by subtracting the number of months and days the infant was born early from the infant's chronological age. The adjusted age should be used to determine both the item set and the Norms Table. In addition, the examiner should be sure to report when adjusted age, rather than chronological age, is used. Differences between adjusted and unadjusted scores can have a significant impact on individual infants because scores are often used to determine eligibility and to evaluate progress in early intervention services.

The use of item sets has also been questioned among infants whose development is atypical, rather than delayed (e.g., an infant with cerebral palsy who has abnormal tone, an infant with autism). The recommendation for most infants is to begin testing with the item set corresponding to the infant's age.

However, in the case of infants with obvious developmental problems, the examiner is advised to begin testing with an item set that approximates the infant's level of functioning. Washington and colleagues (1998) have provided several case studies of full-term infants with atypical development who met basal and ceiling criteria in multiple item sets, with MDI scores that ranged from <50 to 78. These findings illustrate the confusion surrounding the use of item sets among infants with atypical development. Thus strict adherence to item sets may be problematic with premature infants or infants with atypical development because their development is uneven and the concepts of basal and ceiling are too restrictive. Recommendations for testing children with atypical development depend on the reasons for testing (Gyurke & Aylward, 1992). If the examiner wants to compare the results with the standardization sample, then the items should be administered in a standardized manner without adapting the materials or the administration. Standardized testing will yield MDI and PDI scores that can be compared with the standardization sample and used for diagnosis or decision making. On the other hand, if the examiner wants specific information about the infant's skills, then the materials and procedures may be adapted for the specific needs of the infant. These adaptations may help the examiner understand how the infant processes information and handles various problem-solving situations, but MDI and PDI scores cannot be generated and the infant's performance cannot be compared with the standardization sample.

One challenge is how to determine whether the infant's development is proceeding in an even and ordinal fashion and whether the score provides an accurate estimate of the infant's skills. The progression of credits and no credits the infant achieves on the Mental and Motor Scales, in combination with clinical observations of the infant during testing and play, the medical and social history, early intervention experience, the reason for referral, and prior test results (if available), offer some guidance regarding the infant's acquisition of skills. Most infants receive credits for the first items in an item set, followed by a series of credits and no credits for the items in the middle, and no credits for items at the end of the item set. Infants who do not follow this pattern may have uneven or atypical development. In this case, the examiner may want to "test the limits" by testing below the basal or above the ceiling to clarify the infant's strengths and weaknesses.

Infants who exhibit a wide disparity between mental and motor scores (see

Table 5.9, p. 199, of the BSID-II manual) may have uneven or atypical deve opment. The examiner should check the pattern of responses within the Men tal and Motor Scales to check on the pattern of responses. If the progressio of credits and no credits follows the expected pattern, then the concepts o basal and ceiling and item sets included in the BSID-II manual are probabl valid (even if the infant's development is delayed) and the examiner can pro ceed using the standard instructions. On the other hand, if the infant's devel opment is not proceeding in an even and ordinal fashion, the concepts of basal and ceiling may not be valid and the examiner may consider deviating from standard instructions.

Many examiners test the limits of the infant's skills by moving forward and backward through the test by item set or by item. There are no guidelines from the publisher of the BSID-II regarding these nonstandard procedures. Some examiners revert to the basal and ceiling rules from the original BSID and look for sequences of 10 consecutive items passed and 10 consecutive items failed on the Mental Scale (6 consecutive items passed and 6 consecutive items failed on the Motor Scale). However, many infants with atypical development have such uneven profiles that it is difficult to meet the criteria of 10 consecutive items passed and 10 consecutive items failed. Other examiners look for sequences of items passed and failed by area. However, "areas" are not well defined in the BSID-II, and there are no guidelines to indicate how many items passed and failed are needed to reach a criterion of basal and ceiling in each area. This problem has been a primary source of concern in the literature (Ross & Lawson, 1997; Washington et al., 1998) with no satisfactory resolution.

When testing infants with atypical development, many examiners use a two-stage process. In the first stage, they administer the BSID-II adhering to standards and use the resulting score to determine the infant's MDI and PDI. Scores are often needed to track development, to advocate for services, and so on. In the second stage, examiners "test the limits" by using clinical judgment to modify the materials and the test administration to gain information on the infant's strengths and weaknesses. For example, examiners may administer items below the basal or above the ceiling. Information gained from the second stage of testing is incorporated into the report to be used for intervention planning, but it is not used to determine the infant's MDI or PDI. Examiners who choose to deviate from standard procedures should be well rained in infant development and able to defend the conclusions made about the infant's performance. In the report, examiners should be sure to explain how they have modified the standard procedures. This two-stage process enables the examiner to use the information from the first stage to compare the infant's scores with scores of other infants, and to use the information from the second stage to provide specific information on the information processing and learning strategies used by the infant.

Examiners may also use more specific tests that may have been developed specifically for infants with a particular disorder or pattern of development. Infants with disabilities that require test adaptation (e.g., infants with visual, auditory, language, or neuromotor problems) are often better served by more narrow-band, diagnostic tests. However, caution is warranted because many of the specific tests are not well normed.

Other investigators (Washington et al., 1998) have recommended that alternative administrative and scoring procedures be considered. If the BSID-II is going to meet its objective of the "clinical appraisal of high risk and developmentally delayed infants" (Bayley, 1993, p. iii), there is a need for more discussion on the use of the BSID-II among premature infants and infants with delayed and atypical development.

USE OF THE BSID-II WITH INFANTS WITH SPECIAL NEEDS

Validity of the BSID-II is partially demonstrated by eight clinical samples: infants born prematurely, infants who are HIV positive, infants with prenatal substance exposure, birth asphyxia, Down syndrome, autism, developmental delay, and otitis media. The data from the clinical samples demonstrate that the BSID-II can identify developmental delays. Consistent with expectations, infants with developmental delay or Down syndrome have the most depressed MDI and PDI scores, and infants with otitis media had mean MDI and PDI scores within one standard deviation of the mean. The BRS Motor Quality factor received the most Non-Optimal scores among the clinical samples.

The clinical samples are small, and the criteria for inclusion are not well defined. The groups are samples of convenience provided for demonstration. Therefore the data cannot be used to generalize to other samples of infants with similar clinical conditions and cannot serve as a reference for an individ-

≡ *Rapid Reference*

5.2 Strengths and Weaknesses in Facets, BRS, and Training of Examiners

Strengths

- The use of facets attempt to provide information on Motor, Cognitive, Language, and Social Scales.
- The BRS is significantly improved, including inclusion of two parent-report items on infant's performance.
- There are better explanations for BRS items than in previous Infant Behavior Record.
- The BSID-II is only sold to qualified examiners.
- The Psychological Corporation has customer service and a nationwide network of representatives who can assist with questions regarding the BSID-II.

Weaknesses

- There is very weak coverage of the social facet—only three items beyond 4-month level.
- Transferring scores to front of BRS Record Form can be awkward.
- There are minimal explanations for some behavioral anchors in BRS (e.g., frenetic movement, how to test tone).
- BSID-II test kit, Record Forms, and replacement materials are expensive.
- There are no training materials or training criteria to ensure the test is administered appropriately.

ual infant with a particular condition (e.g., prematurity). Furthermore, the data from each clinical sample are presented in aggregate form and there is no discussion of the administrative issues regarding use of item sets with individual infants. Further research is needed to investigate the pattern of BSID-II scores among infants with other disorders.

PREDICTIVE VALIDITY

Bayley and Schaefer (1964) demonstrated that among normal children, there was limited predictability from infant assessment to childhood IQ, largely because there are so many factors that influence early development. Item and factor analyses of the original BSID have shown that not only does the factor structure vary across ages, but there is very little predictability from 3 to 24 months (Burns et al., 1992).

Given the length of time it takes to gather longitudinal data, most new tests do not include data on predictive validity, and the BSID-II is no exception. Predictive validity increases as infants move beyond the sensorimotor stage of development and the cognitive processes (e.g., perceptual discrimination, visual-motor integration) that are measured are more consistent with those that underlie later cognitive and academic performance (Kopp & McCall, 1982). With the extension of the norms of the BSID-II up to 42 months, it is likely that predictive validity will be addressed in future investigations.

BEHAVIOR RATING SCALE

The BRS is a major improvement of the BSID-II. The BRS provides scores on domains that were empirically derived (Motor Quality, Arousal/Attention, Orientation/Engagement, and Emotional Regulation). The BRS also addresses the need to consider differences in developmentally appropriate behavior across the broad age range that the BSID-II assesses. The first two items on the BRS (parent report on the infant's behavior and performance) are particularly useful because they aid the examiner in determining the validity of the evaluation. In addition, the BRS includes better descriptions of the behavioral ratings than its predecessor, the Infant Behavior Record.

The BRS could be improved by more detailed instructions (e.g., how to test muscle tone) and strengthening the descriptions in the manual of some of the behaviors. In addition, transferring the scores from the inside of the Record Form to the face sheet is awkward, time consuming, and increases the likelihood of errors. (See Rapid Reference 5.2.)

TRAINING

The BSID-II is designed to evaluate the mental, motor, and behavioral capabilities of infants through the first 3½ years of life. The items can be administered in a flexible format that facilitates infants' performance and maximizes the likelihood of obtaining a valid assessment. However, the flexibility necessary to administer the BSID-II requires highly skilled examiners who are well trained both in infant development and in the administration of the BSID-II. The Psychological Corporation acknowledges that examiners should have experience and training in testing infants, but there are no specific training guidelines, training materials, or certification procedures. In this regard, the BSID-II is similar to other standardized tests that are manufactured by the Psychological Corporation, such as the Wechsler Scales. Examiners are referred to the *Standards for Educational and Psychological Testing* (American Psychological Association, 1985) or state disciplinary licensing boards for guidelines to examiner qualifications. Yet many BSID-II examiners are not psychologists and not licensed by a state disciplinary licensing board. At least one infant assessment, the Neonatal Behavioral Assessment Scale, includes training and certification procedures that are coordinated by an international network of trainers and certification sites, headquartered at the Brazelton Institute at the Children's Hospital in Boston.

Bayley examiners come from a wide array of disciplinary backgrounds (e.g., psychology, occupational and physical therapy, special education). They should be adequately trained in infant development, standardized assessment, and in the procedures of the BSID-II. Training for the BSID-II should include lectures, demonstrations, and reading assignments, followed by opportunities for trainees to test approximately 10 "practice" infants. Watching and critiquing videotaped administrations of the BSID-II can be an effective training strategy. New examiners should be closely supervised and have opportunities to observe experienced examiners and to be observed by experienced examiners. It is often beneficial and cost efficient to train new BSID-II examiners in pairs. Both new examiners are present with the infant and caregiver. One examiner administers the items and the other examiner records and scores the infant's responses. Following the administration, the two examiners compare notes, thus affording opportunities for both to review the manual and to agree on administration procedures, scoring decisions, and clinical interpretations that can be verified with a supervisor. A second effective training strategy is to videotape the administration of the new examiner administering the BSID-II. The videotape can be reviewed with a supervisor to improve clinical skills and to ensure that the administration, scoring, and interpretation are correct. A third option is to have a supervisor observe the administration of the BSID-II either in the room or behind a one-way mirror. To ensure that scoring is done in a consistent and accurate manner, examiners (new and experienced examiner or two new examiners) should calculate their interrater reliability coefficient. Two examiners score the infant's responses independently and then calculate their level of agreement (reliability coefficient):

CAUTION

5.1 Ensuring the Validity of the BSID-II

- The test materials are copyrighted and cannot be copied or distributed (with the exception of placing a copy of the Record Form in the infant's medical or school record). Adhere to standards set forth in the *Standards for Educational and Psychological Testing* (American Psychological Association, 1985).
- Do not give the Record Form or the test materials to caregivers.
- Although repeated administrations of the BSID-II should not significantly alter an infant's scores, training an infant or encouraging a caregiver to train an infant for the BSID-II will invalidate the score.
- Results of the administration of the BSID-II should be integrated with other information regarding the infant (e.g., birth history, findings from other examiners) and interpreted to the caregivers.

$$\frac{\text{Number of agreements}}{\text{Number of agreements} + \text{Number of disagreements}}$$

The closer the level of agreement is to 1.00, the better the agreement between the two examiners. Disagreements should be discussed and the procedure should be repeated until the level of agreement approaches 1.00 (>0.9). This step is important whether the BSID-II is used as a clinical or a research tool. See Caution 5.1 for guidelines to ensure the validity of the BSID-II.

ADMINISTRATION AND SCORING DIRECTIONS

The administration and scoring directions for the BSID-II items are much more detailed than the directions for the BSID. The precision of the instructions aids in reliability, but requires extensive training.

The directions are enhanced by pictures of the materials needed to administer each item. The pictures and detailed instructions are particularly useful for new examiners getting acquainted with the BSID-II (see Rapid Reference 5.3). However, over time some materials may have to be substituted by the publisher because the manufacturer no longer supplies the original material. In these cases, the picture no longer exactly matches what is in the kit. For

≡ *Rapid Reference*

5.3 Strengths and Weaknesses of Instructions for BSID-II

Strengths

- Each item instruction in the manual includes a picture of the test materials and information on administration and scoring, with extra notes on scoring, administration, and placement in series, as applicable.
- Most instructions are clearly presented and provide much detail.
- Item order on the Record Forms is the same as the order in the manual.
- Record Forms include comprehensive information that facilitates learning how to administer items.
- Cue Sheets provide recommended order of administration.
- Concept of item sets designed to facilitate administration and to reduce the number of items necessary for basal and ceiling.

Weaknesses

- On the Motor Scale, there is no difference in the drawing for Item 31 (partial thumb opposition to grasp cube) and Item 37 (pads of fingertips to grasp cube).
- Instructions for Motor Item 92 (tactilely discriminates shapes) should include ensuring that infant's arm is supinated (palm up).
- Can be difficult to use Record Forms because item order differs from suggested order of administration.
- Use of item sets can become confusing with infants who have atypical development.

example, the squeaky toy has had to be replaced. The replacement material is as similar as possible to the original to maintain the standardization.

TEST KIT MATERIALS

The BSID-II kit is much more organized than the BSID. The kit is a soft-sided luggage case that holds two large plastic containers with dividers and lids and specific compartments for the materials. Labels are provided to mark the location of the materials and to facilitate the organization of the kit. However, part of the "cost" for this improvement is a kit that is very heavy and awkward to carry. Examiners who have to transport kits to satellite locations or to homes

≡ Rapid Reference

5.4 Strengths and Weaknesses in the BSID-II Materials

Strengths

- The kit is well organized with specific locations and labels for test materials.
- Many materials can be washed with bleach and water.
- There is reduced gender and racial bias for many items (e.g., doll, verbal comprehension).
- There is improvement in some manipulatives (e.g., cannot bite pieces from ball or rabbit).
- Items are relatively attractive without being too captivating.
- Round containers are made of solid plastic.
- Materials are designed to be administered in clinics, homes, hospitals, etc.

Weaknesses

- The test kit is very heavy and awkward to carry.
- Replacement items are very expensive.
- Some items retain cultural bias (e.g., "Easter" bunny).
- Shield used for tactile discrimination (Motor Scale Item 92) is very sharp; puzzle pieces split apart.
- Picture of "book" in Stimulus Booklet is confusing because it has a house on the cover.
- Object tray and five items are very unstable (Mental Scale Item 118).
- Doll can be dismembered relatively easily.
- Map in Mental Scale Item 171 is confusing.

sometimes purchase small luggage carts. The square cubes are tightly packed in their container, making it difficult to remove them quickly during testing. Examiners often remove the materials they need prior to testing. See Rapid Reference 5.4 for a list of strengths and weaknesses in the materials.

The materials have been modernized to reduce gender and racial bias and to facilitate washing, in keeping with concerns about infection control. Despite the attention to reduce bias, there is at least one item in the kit that reflects a cultural bias—an "Easter" bunny.

Manipulative Materials

Some of the BSID-II manipulatives are more durable than those in the BSID. For example, infants can no longer take bites out of the ball or rabbit.

On the other hand, the cups break easily and the puzzle pieces often come apart at the seam.

Although most of the materials for the BSID-II are well designed and attractive, there are some that are problematic. The plastic shield used for tactile discrimination (Motor Scale Item 92) has a sharp edge that gets placed over the infant's arm. Many infants are frightened by having to place their arm under the shield. (The administration of this item might have been easier and less frightening to the infant if the directions had instructed the examiner to place the item to be manipulated in a bag so that the infant could feel the item inside the bag.) The clear box that is used as a barrier to retrieve a toy (Mental Scale Items 88 and 105) may begin to crack under the pressure of infants who try to wrest it from the examiner's hands rather than reach through the open side. Once it cracks, it should be replaced immediately because the sharp edges could cut an infant. Also, the mirror has a plastic, red protective strip that draws the infant's attention and comes off easily when taking the mirror out of the kit.

The replacement materials for the BSID-II are very expensive, and a few materials must be replaced often, such as the pellets. Many of the replacement materials are sold in sets, rather than as single items so the examiner has to pay for materials not needed. Examiners who might try to economize by upgrading the BSID to the BSID-II soon learn that purchasing the new items costs more than buying an entire kit.

Printed Materials

The manual is bound in a soft cover that tears easily. In addition, pages soon begin to fall out. One suggestion is to make a copy of the pages that are used repeatedly (e.g., norms tables, cue sheets) and place them in a separate binder. The items in the manual are presented in an ordinal sequence that matches the order on the Record Forms. In most cases, the instructions are clear and comprehensive. However, there are several areas where caution is warranted. The drawings for Motor Scale Item 31 (partial thumb opposition to grasp cube) and Item 37 (pads of finger tips to grasp cube) appear to be the same. Item 31 occurs earlier in development than Item 37 and the distinction would have been clearer if the drawing had focused on the partial thumb opposition and the drawing for Item 37 had focused on the fingers. In addition, the administration directions of Motor Scale Item 92 (Tactilely Discriminates Shapes) could be improved if the manual were to instruct the examiner to ensure that the infant's arm was supinated (palm up) so that the examiner could drop the object to be felt into the infant's hand. If the child's hand is pronated (palm down), the tendons are stretched, making it awkward for the infant to grasp and feel objects.

The Record Forms can be difficult to use during testing because the items are not in the order in which they are typically administered. One option is to copy the Cue Sheets and to make notes regarding the infant's responses during testing that are then transferred to the Record Forms during breaks or following testing. Another option that has been used by some examiners is to create an alternate Record Form to conform to the order of administration found on the Cue Sheets. This process would be facilitated if examiners had a choice of purchasing Record Forms either in ordinal sequence or in recommended order of administration. Clinicians might prefer the Record Forms in ordinal sequence to aid in the analysis of the infant's pattern of responses. Researchers, who are often less concerned about clinical interpretations, might prefer the Record Forms in recommended order of administration to ensure consistent administrative procedures, particularly when infants of the same age are being evaluated.

The Stimulus Booklet is used for the administration of many items and thus gets much use. The illustrations that appear on the pages of the Stimulus Booklet are attractive and almost all of them appear in multiple colors. Unfortunately, the first two pages get quickly worn and torn. In lieu of purchasing another Stimulus Booklet, the examiner may laminate these pages. Another annoyance concerning the Stimulus Booklet is that the binding begins to "walk," and from time to time the examiner needs to thread it back through the holes of the pages of the Stimulus Booklet.

SUMMARY

Although the BSID-II is an excellent revision of the BSID, there are small errors in the manual and there are improvements that would make the test even better. A major consideration is the applicability of the test to populations

≡ *Rapid Reference*

5.5 Recommendations to Consider in the Next Revision of the BSID

- Area scores should be consistent with IDEA: Cognitive, Motor, Communication, Social, and Adaptive.
- Reconsider concept of item sets and criteria for basal and ceiling with recognition that Bayley Scales are often used to evaluate infants with delayed and atypical development.
- Accommodations for evaluating infants with special needs must be addressed.
- Consideration for testing infants from non-English-speaking families should be addressed. In the United States a Spanish version should be developed so that infants of Spanish-speaking families may be assessed.
- Criteria for translating and adapting Bayley Scales for use in non-U.S. cultures should be addressed.
- Criteria for training examiners should be included.
- The materials must be updated to facilitate portability and incorporate the suggestions regarding clarity of administration.

that were not represented within the standardization sample (infants from non-English-speaking families and from other countries). In addition, as with all standardized assessments, over time the standardization sample will no longer be representative of the U.S. population, so the norms will need to be updated (Flynn, 1999). Suspected errors or questions about the BSID-II should be directed to the Psychological Corporation. Recommendations for the next revision of the BSID are included in Rapid Reference Box 5.5.

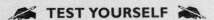

TEST YOURSELF

1. **The normative range for the BSID-II is**
   (a) 2– 30 months.
   (b) 1–42 months.
   (c) 1–12 months.
   (d) 1–60 months.

2. **Examiners should give caregivers materials from the BSID-II so that they can train their infants and improve their performance.** True or False?

3. **The BSID-II should only be administered by a trained and experienced examiner.** True or False?

4. **BSID examiners who want to upgrade to the BSID-II should**
   (a) order replacement parts from the Psychological Corporation.
   (b) purchase toys that resemble those in the BSID-II.
   (c) order a new kit from the Psychological Corporation.
   (d) continue to use the BSID and estimate the infant's performance on the BSID-II.

5. **BSID-II examiners**
   (a) must be trained and certified by the Psychological Corporation.
   (b) should be knowledgeable in infant development and trained in the administration, scoring, and interpretation of the BSID-II.
   (c) can usually train themselves by studying the BSID-II manual.
   (d) all of the above

6. **The norms on the BSID-II can be used for infants from any country.** True or False?

7. **An examiner who discovers a possible mistake in the BSID-II manual should**
   (a) do nothing; the manual is published and mistakes cannot be corrected.
   (b) contact the Psychological Corporation.
   (c) contact a lawyer.
   (d) make the correction in the manual.

8. **The new items in the BSID-II do not need to be washed because they are infection resistant.** True or False?

continued

9. **If an item from the BSID-II is lost, replacement items that are similar to the original items can be purchased from a local store.** True or False?

10. **If an infant is not acquiring developmental skills in an ordinal sequence, the examiner should use the BSID-II to establish MDI and PDI scores and then test the limits of the infant's skills by administering items beyond the ceiling and below the basal.** True or False?

11. **If the examiner tests the limits by administering items above the ceiling or below the basal and includes those items in the calculation of the raw score, the Norms Tables are no longer valid.** True or False?

12. **A 20-month infant is referred for evaluation due to concerns about language development. The examiner begins with the 20- to 22-month item set and the infant establishes a basal and a ceiling within that item set. The infant does not make any verbalizations. What does the examiner do?**

   (a) The examiner reports the infant's scores from the 20- to 22-month item set because the infant has satisfied basal and ceiling criteria.

   (b) The examiner administers the 17- to 19-month item set because the referral question concerned language and the examiner suspects that the infant would not receive credit for all items in 17- to 19-month item set. If the infant establishes a basal in the 17- to 19-month item set, the examiner reports the basal from the 17- to 19-month item set and the ceiling from the 20- to 22-month item set.

   (c) As above, the examiner administers the 17- to 19-month item set but does not report the scores because the infant met basal and ceiling criteria in the 20- to 22-month item set.

   (d) The examiner administers only the language items from the 17- to 19-month item set and reports approximated index and developmental age scores.

Answers: 1. b; 2. False; 3. True; 4. c; 5. b; 6. False; 7. b; 8. False; 9. False; 10. True; 11. True; 12. b

Six

CLINICAL APPLICATIONS OF THE BSID-II

The revision of the Bayley Scales acknowledged a major shift in the purpose of infant assessment (see Rapid Reference 6.1). When Nancy Bayley published the original scale, her emphasis was on normal development and the Bayley Scales were "designed to provide adequate measurement of the developmental progress of infants, both for clinical and research use" (1969, p. iii). The BSID quickly became the assessment of choice to describe infant development.

By the time the revision to the Bayley Scales was published 24 years later, the country was in the midst of the early intervention movement. As Jane V. Hunt wrote in the preface to the revision, "The purpose of infant assessment has shifted from the evaluation of normal infants to the clinical appraisal of high risk and developmentally delayed infants" (Bayley, 1993, p. iii). In this chapter we present recent examples of how the BSID has contributed to the science and practice of infant development. Specifically, we examine how the BSID has been used in early intervention, with children who have chronic illnesses and other special health care needs, and with children undergoing medical and surgical procedures. We also briefly review the limited research that has been conducted with the BSID-II since its publication in 1993.

INFANCY RESEARCH

Since the publication of the BSID in 1969, multiple factors have in-

═══ *Rapid Reference*
....

6.1 Purpose of the Bayley Scales

- BSID: Provides adequate measurement of the developmental progress of infants
- BSID-II: Clinically appraises high risk and developmentally delayed infants

≡ *Rapid Reference*
....

6.2 Factors That Influence the Science and Practice of Infant Development

- Interest in normal infant development
- Survival of premature and low-birth-weight infants
- Expanded conceptualization of the role that environmental conditions and caregiving practices play in infant development
- Early intervention movement

fluenced the science and practice of infant development (see Rapid Reference 6.2). The first factor was the burgeoning interest in normal infant development that flourished during the 1960s and 1970s and gave rise to much research in infancy using the BSID. Developmentalists investigated the course of normal development and developmental psychopathologists and clinicians investigated disruptions to the developmental process and strategies for recovery. Both researchers and clinicians used the BSID to describe individual differences in infants' mental and motor development and contributed many advances to the understanding of infants' abilities to self-regulate and to process information. Clinicians, such as T. Berry Brazelton, M.D., worked to translate the research into practice and to dispel the myth that infants were unsophisticated organisms who could not process information or respond to their environment. Researchers and clinicians (many of whom used the BSID) demonstrated the processing capabilities of infants. As these skills became known to the public, an industry emerged that produced books, toys, and products to stimulate infants and to maximize their early development. The BSID contributed to a broader conceptualization of infants' skills by documenting the systematic changes that occur throughout the first few years of life.

An increase in the survival rate of premature and low-birth-weight infants over the past 20 years is the second factor that influenced the science and practice of infant development. Advances in the management of high-risk pregnancies and neonatal intensive care led to the viability of younger and smaller infants (Hack & Fanaroff, 1988). However, follow-up studies have shown that premature and low-birth-weight infants are at increased risk for long-term developmental problems that can compromise their ability to learn and to achieve during school-aged years (Hack et al., 1994). Although species-specific maturation and self-righting tendencies may minimize the threat of challenges during early development (McCall, 1981), many high-risk infants are unable to recover and do not achieve the expected developmental skills. For example, in a follow-up of extremely low birth weight infants (<1,001 grams), Messinger, Dolcourt, King, Bodnar, and Beck (1996) reported on the BSID scores of 34 infants conducted at 18 months of age. Although a majority of the infants achieved MDI scores in the normal range (≥85), 15% had scores that were slightly delayed (MDI between 70 and 84), and 21% had scores that were substantially delayed (MDI scores below 70). Infants who had a history of intraventricular hemorrhage (Grade III or IV) were most likely to have lower MDI scores. The wide deviation of the scores (mean = 88.63, standard deviation = 21.75) illustrates the diversity among the infants' skills.

The third factor to influence the science and practice of infant development is the broadened conceptualization of infant development that has emerged over time. Transactional, ecological models of development replaced maturational models, and social and environmental variables, such as the quality of the home and relationships with family members were recognized as important components of infant development (Bronfenbrenner, 1979; Sameroff & Chandler, 1975). The influence of social and environmental variables was incorporated into the early intervention movement and led to the development of family-oriented programs for infants who were at risk for developmental delay due to prematurity or poverty, as well as infants with disabilities (e.g., cerebral palsy) (Guralnick, 1996; Shonkoff, Hauser-Cram, Krauss, & Upshur, 1992). Changes in infants' motor or cognitive development were often evaluated by the BSID.

The emphasis on social and environmental influences on infant development has even extended to neonatal intensive care units. Using a phase lag design, Als (1997) evaluated the impact of family-centered, developmentally supportive models of care on early infant development. She reported that among infants born at very low birth weight (<1,250 grams), those in the experimental condition (relationship-based, individualized developmental approach) had higher MDI and PDI scores at 18 months than infants in the control condition (traditional task and teaching-oriented approach). Findings linking the environment and caregiving practices with developmental performance have been instrumental in altering practices and conditions in nurseries and neonatal intensive care units.

The final factor that influenced the science and practice of infant development is the early intervention movement, which emerged following the recognition that infant development could be influenced by environmental conditions and caregiving practices. Early intervention programs were designed to promote normal development, to ensure that disruptions to the developmental process are minimized, to prevent subsequent learning and academic problems, and to support families in their mission of providing protection and nurturance to their infants (Coie et al., 1993; Guralnick, 1996). The BSID has played a major role by enabling researchers and clinicians to describe the course of normal development, to track the progress of individual infants during early intervention, and to evaluate the efficacy of intervention strategies.

EARLY INTERVENTION

Early intervention has attracted much national attention in recent years as scientists, health providers, educators, and policy makers discovered what some parents have known for centuries—that the first 3 years of life are a time of rapid change and opportunity in human growth and development (Guralnick, 1996). Infants triple their birth weight in the 1st year of life and by the age of 3 years, they have mastered a wide range of skills and are able to walk, talk, solve basic problems, and form close relationships. Much of the longitudinal research that has demonstrated the importance of the first 3 years of life for the formation of cognitive, language, motor, and emotional skills has relied on the BSID as a psychometrically valid measure of children's development (e.g., Belsky, 1984; Burchinal et al., 1997).

Early intervention programs address two broad risk categories: environmental and biological. Despite the increased incidence of premature and low-birth-weight births, the most formidable challenge to children's development is poverty (Klerman, 1991). National data indicate that over 20% of the children in the United States live in poverty, with rates rising to 50% among infants under age 3 from ethnic minority families (National Commission on Children, 1991). Environmental challenges associated with poverty, including limited access to appropriate developmental challenges and stimulation, often result in low scores on the Bayley Scales (Bradley et al., 1994).

Biological risks extend beyond prematurity and low birth weight to include chronic health or disabling conditions that undermine infants' development, such as cerebral palsy (Aylward, Peiffer, Wright, & Verhulst, 1989; Mc-Cormick, 1989). All too often, environmental and biological risks co-occur because infants in low-income families are more vulnerable to biological challenges, such as prematurity.

The BSID has played a prominent role in the evaluation of many early intervention programs designed to remediate both environmental and biological risks. Although the field of early intervention has been plagued by methodological problems that hinder program evaluation, including lack of randomized assignment, small sample sizes, biased examiners, cost factors, and inadequate analytic techniques (Black, 1991), there are many examples of well-evaluated programs, many of which have used the BSID. For example, Burchinal and colleagues (1997) recently reported on the long-term effects of two early intervention programs (the Abecedarian Project and Project CARE) designed to promote development among infants and young children from low-income families. During infancy and preschool years the Abecedarian Project examined center-based child care versus no child care, and Project CARE compared home visiting with and without center-based child care versus no child care. The children who received early child care achieved higher MDI scores on the BSID at 12, 18, and 24 months, and higher IQ scores at 36, 42, 48, 54, 60, 78, and 96 months than those who received home visiting only or those in no-treatment groups (see Figure 6.1). In addition, at 18 months of age, infants who received early child care had greater increases and higher scores on task performance (measured by the Infant Behavior Record of the BSID) than infants in other groups. Although there was an overall decline in cognitive performance over the 8-year study period, children had better performance when they received early child care, and had a responsive home environment and a mother with a higher IQ.

It is not unusual for infants raised in low-income families to experience a general decline in cognitive scores over the first several years of life (Burchinal et al., 1997). As the maturational unfolding of early infancy is replaced by the increasingly important role of environmental influences, individual differences

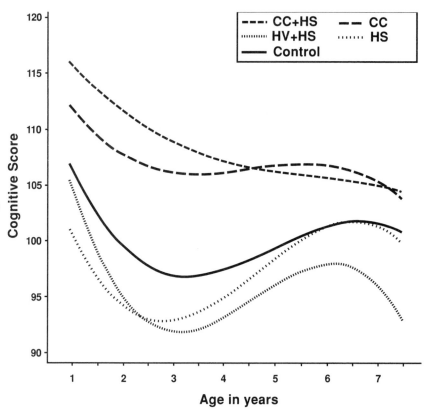

Figure 6.1 Growth Curves of Cognitive Performance Scores by Intervention Groups

Note. CC, Child Care; HS, Home-School; HV, Home Visit. From "Early intervention and mediating processes in cognitive performance of children of low-income African-American families," by M. R. Burchinal, F. A. Campbell, D. M. Bryant, B. H. Wasik, and C. T. Ramey, 1997, Child Development, 68, pp. 935–954. Copyright © 1997 by Blackwell. Reproduced with permission. All rights reserved.

in development are accentuated, often with sharp declines in developmental progress among children from low-income families and communities. Thus early intervention programs often attempt to slow down or to reverse the developmental decline typically experienced by children raised in poverty.

A reduction in the rate of developmental decline was demonstrated when the BSID was used to evaluate early home-based intervention programs among low-income infants with nonorganic failure to thrive. Infants who received home intervention for one year showed less decline in cognitive development (measured by the BSID) and more enriched home environments than those in the comparison group (Black, Dubowitz, Hutcheson, Berenson-Howard, & Starr, 1995).

BEHAVIOR AND DEVELOPMENTAL ASPECTS OF CHRONIC ILLNESSES

The BSID has been used to track the cognitive and motor developmental course of children exposed to infectious diseases and chronic illnesses, such as HIV infection. Pediatric HIV infection is caused by vertical transmission of HIV infection from mothers to their newborn infants. The BSID has been used to examine the impact of HIV infection on infants' early development. HIV-infected infants have lower MDI scores than seroreverting infants (infants born to HIV-positive mothers who did not contract the infection) from investigations conducted in the United States (Mellins, Levenson, Zawadzki, Kairam, & Weston, 1994) and Uganda (Drotar et al., 1999). The MDI scores of seroreverting infants did not differ from scores of infants of drug-abusing women (Mellins et al., 1994) or scores of infants from non-infected women (Drotar et al., 1999). These findings demonstrate the use of the BSID to assess the effects of HIV infection on early cognitive development in the United States and in Uganda. The BSID may also be used to track the developmental progress of HIV-infected infants in response to alternative treatment options.

The impact of prenatal exposure to substances has attracted national attention with the epidemic of substance use (especially cocaine) among women of child-bearing age. Studies conducted during the neonatal period suggest that there are transitional effects of prenatal cocaine exposure on infant development that are often resolved by 4 to 6 weeks of age (Black, Schuler, & Nair, 1993; Coles, Platzman, Smith, James, & Falek, 1992). However, follow-up studies with the BSID have led to controversial findings. For example, Hurt, Brodsky, Betancourt, & Braitman (1995) used the BSID to evaluate cocaine-exposed infants and a comparison group of nonexposed infants from the same socioeconomic background at age 30 months. They found that although the scores of both groups were depressed below those in an external comparison group of privately insured infants (see Figure 6.2), the scores of the infants in the two study groups did not differ. The mean MDI score for the

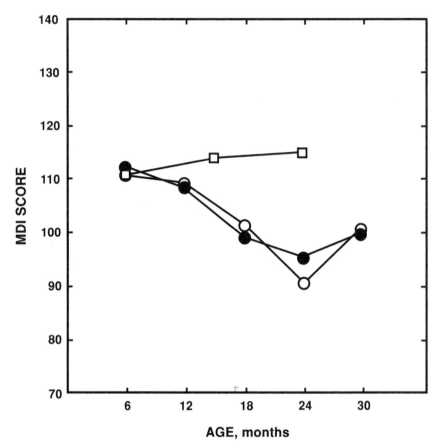

Figure 6.2 BSID MDI Sources of Cocaine-Exposed and Control Children

Note. BSID MDI scores of cocaine-exposed (●) and control (O) children at each follow-up visit.
(□) is composed of full-term, primarily white, privately insured children. From "Cocaine-exposed children: Follow-up through 30 months," by H. Hurt, N. L. Brodsky, L. Betancourt, and L. E. Braitman, 1995, *Journal of Developmental and Behavioral Pediatrics*, 16, pp. 291–35. Copyright © 1995 by Lippincott Williams & Wilkins. Reproduced with permission. All rights reserved.

infants in the privately insured group was above 110, reflecting the inflation that has occurred in MDI scores over time. The mean MDI and PDI scores for the infants in the cocaine-exposed and comparison groups were closer to 100. In contrast, Arendt and colleagues (1998) found lower performance on the BSID MDI and PDI scores among cocaine exposed infants at age 12-months, in comparison with nonexposed infants. The lack of consensus in this research verifies the methodological challenges in substance abuse research. Not only is it difficult to quantify prenatal substance exposure, but there may be other social and environmental factors, beyond prenatal substance exposure, that contribute to early infant development, as shown by the overall depression in scores at 30 months (Hurt et al., 1995).

The BSID has also been used with infants who have significant sensory impairments. For example, Leguire, Fellows, and Bier (1990) tracked the development of infants with severe visual impairments and demonstrated how the MDI could be used to provide information about infants' use of residual vision. This use of the BSID illustrates how examiners can make systematic adaptations to the standard administration procedures to accommodate the needs of infants with specific disabilities, such as visual impairment. The examiners were more interested in the systematic use of the BSID procedures to describe infants' use of residual vision than in the use of standardized scores.

APPLICATION OF THE BSID TO MEDICAL AND SURGICAL PROCEDURES

The BSID has been used in medical settings to examine the impact of surgical procedures on infant development. For example, Bellinger and colleagues (1995) studied the mental and motor development of 155 infants who required cardiac repair during the first three months of life. At age 1, infants who received a low-flow cardiopulmonary bypass had higher PDI scores and fewer neurological abnormalities than infants who received hypothermia and circulatory arrest. The infants tended to have BSID scores that were approximately 0.5 standard deviations below the norm for the MDI and 1.0 standard deviations below the norm for the PDI, consistent with the adverse effects of cardiac abnormalities and corrective surgery on infant development. These findings illustrate not only the importance of having a psychometrically sound measure of infant development, but also the interplay among chronic conditions (e.g., cardiac abnormalities), surgical procedures, and infant development.

NEUROPSYCHOLOGICAL DEVELOPMENT

Developmental neuropsychology is an emerging field that represents the contributions of neurology, developmental psychology, clinical psychology, neuropsychology, pediatrics, and psychiatry, among other fields (Spreen, Risser, & Edgell, 1995). It is concerned with the integration of the brain-behavior relationship within the developing infant and child. With the increasing survival rate of premature infants and infants with complex medical and congenital problems, there is a corresponding need to understand the implications of early central nervous system challenges on the developing infant. The primary emphasis of developmental neuropsychology on developmental change and maturation differentiates it as conceptually different from adult neuropsychology, rather than a subset of adult neuropsychology (Aylward, 1997).

The BSID (and now the BSID-II) is extremely useful in developmental neuropsychological research and practice because it provides a measure of overall infant functioning. In addition, the BSID-II can be considered as a neuropsychological screener because it provides scores in neurological functions (motor development), receptive functions, expressive functions, and cognitive processes (Aylward, 1997).

Examiners who are interested in neuropsychology and want a screening assessment may consider the Bayley Infant Neurodevelopmental Screener (BINS; Aylward, 1995). The BINS assesses neurodevelopment (posture, tone, movement, developmental status, and basic neurological intactness) in infants from 3 to 24 months. It is published by the Psychological Corporation and incorporates items from the BSID-II, but it is not a subset of the BSID-II. The BINS is based on the concept of optimality in which the predictability of early positive outcomes is more accurate than the predictability of early negative outcomes. There are three classification groupings: Low Risk, Moderate Risk, and High Risk. Scoring for the BINS emphasizes the quality of the infant's response and each item is scored as optimal or nonoptimal. There is a high classification agreement between the BINS and the BSID-II.

Infant researchers continue to investigate the intricacies of early development, as applied to typically developing infants and to infants with early biological and environmental challenges. Although the BSID-II plays an important role by describing the higher level functioning of infants in comparison to other infants of the same age and serving as a neuropsychological screener, it was not designed to address the processing questions that are emerging in developmental neuropsychology.

USE OF THE BSID IN NON-U.S. CULTURES

The BSID has been translated and adapted for use in multiple cultures outside the United States. Several investigators have used the BSID or BSID-II to examine the relationship between infants' cognitive development and nutritional status. In Indonesia Humphrey and colleagues (1998) used the BSID-II to evaluate the impact of neonatal vitamin A supplements on children's MDI, PDI, and BRS Scores at 3 years of age. Vitamin A supplementation had a small beneficial (though nonsignificant) effect on MDI and PDI scores and a significant effect on two BRS subscales (Orientation/ Engagement and Motor Quality).

Lozoff, Wolf, and Jimenez (1996) used the BSID to examine the impact of iron-deficiency anemia and iron therapy on the development and behavior of 12- to 23-month-old infants in Costa Rica. They found that infants with iron-deficient anemia had lower MDI scores than nonanemic infants prior to treatment and after 3 and 6 months of iron therapy. There were no group differences in motor scores, but there was a trend toward differences in behavioral scores with anemic infants being more tearful and unhappy. In another investigation, the team used the Infant Behavior Record of the BSID to examine behavioral differences between 12- to 23-month-old infants with and without iron-deficiency anemia (Lozoff et al., 1998). Infants with iron-deficiency anemia had marginally lower scores in overall affect, particularly on the Endurance subscale (42% suspect scores among anemic infants and 19% suspect scores among iron sufficient infants). These findings illustrate the importance of the BSID, particularly the Infant Behavior Record, in providing systematic evaluations of infant development and behavior to examine the impact of iron-deficiency anemia and iron therapy.

In China investigators have used the BSID to examine the effects of prenatal lead exposure and development during the 1st year of life (Shen et al., 1998). Infants were divided into low- or high-lead-level groups based on lead levels obtained from their cord blood. When the BSID was administered at 3, 6, and 12 months, infants in the low-lead group obtained higher MDI scores at each administration (3.4 points at 3 months, 6.3 at 6 months, and 5.2 at 12 months). There were no group differences in motor scores, and MDI scores were related to prenatal lead levels, but not to current lead levels obtained at the time of the evaluations. Thus prenatal lead exposure appears to have a deleterious effect on infants' development through the 1st year of life.

Examiners in India have developed local norms (Baroda norms) for the Indian version of the BSID, together with information on reliability and validity (Phatak, 1993). In India the BSID is used in clinical settings to identify infants with developmental delays or disabilities and in research settings. Examples of the research include the identification of early indicators of developmental delay in high-risk infants (Aggarwal, Chaudhari, Bhave, Pandit, & Barve, 1998; Godbole et al., 1997) and comparisons of the development of twins and singletons (Chaudhari, Bhalerao, Vaidya, Pandit, & Nene, 1997).

In Finland investigators used the BSID to examine differences in early development and temperament between full-term and preterm infants (Sajaniemi, Salokorpi, & von Wendt, 1998). They found that at 2 years of age, preterm infants achieved lower MDI and PDI scores than full-term infants. When Infant Behavior Record scores were considered, preterm infants were less active, more adaptive, more positive, less intense, and lower in threshold to respond than the full-term infants.

Taken together, these studies indicate that the BSID, including the Infant Behavior Record, has been widely used in international investigations to provide new insight into the effects of prematurity, infant health, and nutritional intervention on infant behavior and development. Most investigators have been careful to use local comparison groups and not to make comparisons between local performance and U.S. norms. In addition, many investigators are using the BSID-II and the Behavior Rating Scale. However, most of the international reports using the BSID-II and BRS focused on content, with almost no attention directed to methodological issues on the use of the BSID-II and BRS in non-U.S. cultures.

METHODOLOGICAL ISSUES REGARDING THE BSID

Although most research conducted with the BSID has been content oriented, there have been important methodological studies that have examined the structure of the BSID. For example, Aylward and colleagues (1995) examined MDI and PDI differences among infants at 6, 12, and 24 months of age. They reported that MDI and PDI differences were not related to either socioeconomic status or biological risk (with the exception of 6 months corrected age). However, there was a clear relationship between MDI and PDI differences and the infant's cognitive skills. Regardless of age, at high cognitive levels the MDI was 3 to 14 points higher than the PDI and at low cognitive levels; the PDI was 1.5 to 10 points higher than the MDI. Longitudinal analyses revealed that MDI and PDI differences vary over time, with little stability among infants. Again, patterns of MDI and PDI differences were not predicted by socioeconomic status, biological risk, or gestational age (Aylward et al., 1995). Thus differences scores should be interpreted with caution.

LeTendre and colleagues (1992) found that 73% of the 24-month old infants in their sample did not meet the ceiling criteria of 10 consecutive items failed on the MDI. On the PDI only 5% of the 24-month-old infants did not meet the ceiling criteria of six items failed. Thus the order of item difficulty may vary between the two scales, especially at the upper age levels.

RESEARCH WITH THE BSID-II

The publication of the BSID-II has generated symposia at professional meetings, comments, and empirical investigations of differences between the BSID and BSID-II. Comparisons between the two versions of the Bayley Scales found that infants achieved lower scores on the BSID-II, documenting the importance of updating the norms for scales of infant development (Goldstein et al., 1995; Tasbihsazan et al., 1997).

Most examiners rely on the age-adjusted index scores or developmental age scores of the BSID-II. However, index scores can not be calculated when infants achieve index scores that would be below 50 or above 130. Robinson and Mervis (1996) used statistical procedures to develop extrapolated scores that extend index scores from 50 down to 30. Lindsey and Brouwers (1999) compared two methods for deriving age equivalents from raw scores. The linear method was superior to the regression method and enabled examiners to include scores that extended beyond the age range of the test. (As noted in Chapter 4, examiners who rely on statistical methods to estimate index scores or age equivalents, rather than relying on the Norms Tables, should note that the scores were estimated.)

Many investigators have raised questions regarding the use of the item sets, and basal and ceiling criteria of the BSID-II, particularly among premature infants and those with delayed or atypical development (Gauthier et al., 1999; Matula et al., 1997; Ross & Lawson, 1997; Washington et al., 1998). As noted in Chapter 5, investigators are concerned that the assumption of ordinality that forms the basis for the structure of the BSID (and BSID-II) may jeopardize conclusions made about the developmental profile of infants who have delayed or atypical development. Investigators are committed to the need for systematic, psychometrically sound assessment procedures to identify infants with developmental delays and/or disabilities and to track their developmental progress. Most investigators advocate for continued dialogue among Bayley examiners to define the validity of the test among special populations and for administrative and scoring procedures that provide opportunities to describe the full range of infants' cognitive and motor development.

TEST YOURSELF

1. **The BSID-II should not be used with infants with infectious diseases because they were not included in the standardization sample.** True or False?

2. **Developmental neuropsychology is a downward extension of adult neuropsychology.** True or False?

3. **Which of the following did not influence the early intervention movement?**
   (a) advances in medical technology leading to an increase in the survival rate of premature and low-birth-weight infants
   (b) recognition that environmental and social variables influence infant development
   (c) the BSID as a valid and reliable measure of infant development
   (d) HIV infection in infants

4. **The BSID-II can be considered a developmental neuropsychological screener.** True or False?

5. **The Infant Behavior Record (or BRS) can yield important information about infant behavior, even if there are no findings related to cognitive or motor development.** True or False?

6. **The impact of early intervention programs on infant development cannot be measured by the BSID-II MDI or PDI.** True or False?

7. **The BSID-II can be useful in determining the impact of surgical procedures, such as those used during cardiac repairs, on infant development.** True or False?

8. **Infants are protected from the negative effects of poverty often seen among older children.** True or False?

Answers: 1. False; 2. False; 3. d; 4. True; 5. True; 6. False; 7. True; 8. False

Seven

ILLUSTRATIVE CASE REPORTS

This chapter includes examples of evaluations conducted on four infants. Three were referred for evaluation, and one was evaluated with the BSID-II as part of a research protocol. The purpose of the case reports is to provide specific examples of the use of the BSID-II incorporating the principles of administration, scoring, and interpretation introduced earlier. Note that in the four cases presented, all infants' names have been replaced with pseudonyms to ensure anonymity.

GENERAL GUIDELINES FOR WRITING REPORTS

The report that results from the assessment of the infant's development is often instrumental in determining the infant's diagnosis and need for early intervention services. The examiner should focus on the purpose of the assessment and address the referral questions. Reports should be written in a clear and succinct style, using sentences that are direct. Reports that are long, complex, and include tangential, theoretical discussions are unlikely to be read.

Reports must be accurate and contain information that the examiner can verify. Results should be checked and rechecked to avoid computational errors. Reports should not include gossip or hearsay. Remember that caregivers have the right to read reports. Reports are confidential and cannot be released to anyone other than the referral source without the written permission of the caregivers.

Examiners should avoid making long-term predictions based on tests given during infancy. The predictive validity of the BSID-II (and other infant tests) is low. Reports often follow children for many years through the educational and health care systems.

The BSID-II provides important information on an infant's response to a structured testing situation. However, the results should not be interpreted in isolation. They should be integrated with the infant's medical and social history, along with observations, information from the caregiver, and reports from other clinicians.

Reports often include six sections: Identifying Information, Reason for Referral, Background, Appearance and Behavioral Observations, Testing Results, and Summary and Recommendations. Don't Forget 7.1 through 7.6, spaced throughout this chapter, provide additional guidelines on preparing a report.

Case I: Karla J.

	Score	*Category*
BRS	91st percentile	Within Normal Limits
MDI	89	Within Normal Limits
PDI	82	Mildly Delayed Performance

Reason for Referral

Karla's age is 13 months, 8 days. She was referred for evaluation by her pediatrician because her growth is faltering, and there are concerns about her development and about her eligibility for early intervention.

DON'T FORGET

7.1 Information to Include in the Identifying Information Section of a Report

- Infant's name
- Names of parents
- Date of birth
- Date of evaluation
- Age of infant
- Name of examiner

Background

Karla was born at 38 weeks gestation. Her birth weight of 2,750 grams and length of 49.5 centimeters (6 pounds, 1 ounce, 19½ inches) were appropriate for gestational age. There were no neonatal concerns and she was discharged after 2 days. For the first 8 months, her growth was Within Normal Limits and there were no medical or developmental concerns. Between 8 and 12 months, however,

Karla's weight gain slowed, and at her 12-month checkup, her weight for age had dropped to below the 5th percentile based on national standards. There were no medical explanations for her delayed growth. Her pediatrician administered the Denver II and noted that Karla failed several motor and language items. A referral was made for a developmental evaluation to determine if Karla was eligible to receive early intervention services.

Karla lives with her mother, her maternal grandmother, and her mother's two teenaged siblings. Karla's mother is 18 years of age, dropped out of school in the 11th grade, and is currently unemployed. Karla's father visits once or twice a month. He brings diapers but does not provide regular child support and is no longer involved with Karla's mother. Karla's grandmother works as a licensed practical nurse to support the family. Karla receives WIC and medical assistance. The family lives in a very low income neighborhood and Karla's mother and grandmother both commented on the ever-present dangers and unfriendliness of the neighbors. They do not participate in church or community activities.

> ### DON'T FORGET
>
> **7.2 Information to Include in the Reason for Referral Section of a Report**
>
> - Reason that the infant is being evaluated—what questions are to be addressed
> - Who made the referral—include name, address, phone number
> - Concerns expressed by the parents or caregivers
> - Current medical concerns or disabilities (e.g., cerebral palsy)

Karla's early developmental history is not remarkable. Her mother reported that she adjusted easily to the household routine and was sleeping through the night by 3 months of age. She was bottle-fed and was an enthusiastic feeder until about 4 months of age when her mother began to give her pureed foods. Karla rejected the pureed foods by spitting and turning her head. Karla's mother sometimes forced her to eat by squeezing her cheeks and holding her mouth. Feeding has continued to be a source of frustration. Karla readily drinks from a bottle but frequently refuses to accept table food and rarely requests food.

Appearance and Behavioral Observations

Karla presented as an attractive, well-groomed, neatly dressed child who appeared younger than her age of 13 months. Her weight for age, height for age, and weight for height were all below the 5th percentile. Karla was accompanied by her mother and grandmother. Karla's grandmother answered most of the questions and was clearly in charge. She denied concerns about Karla's growth or development and expressed some irritation at having to take off work for the appointment. Karla sat on her grandmother's lap with a pacifier in her mouth.

During the testing session, Karla sat at a child-sized table and chairs. She demonstrated an age-appropriate level of cooperation and attention and was not easily distracted. She seemed to enjoy the individual attention. On several occasions she looked to her grandmother, who repeatedly told her to "play with the doctor." Karla's mother sat to the side and did not interact with Karla or with her mother.

Karla's grandmother reported that her behavior on the test was atypical because she was more compliant and cooperative than she is at home. She also commented that she had no idea that Karla could do so many things. The BSID-II was regarded as a valid estimation of Karla's skills because she was so cooperative during testing, her performance was very consistent (pattern of credits, followed by credits and no credits intermixed, followed by no credits), and her grandmother reported that while her performance was somewhat atypical, it was more optimal than usual and her behavior was excellent.

Results

On the BRS Karla obtained an overall score at the 91st percentile, which is Within Normal Limits. In Orientation/Engagement, Emotional Regulation, and Motor Quality she obtained scores at the 85th, 82nd, and 99th percentiles, respectively, all Within Normal Limits.

The 13-month item set was administered for the Mental and Motor Scales and was scored as follows:

13-Month Item Set—Mental Scale
Credit: Items 78, 79, 80, 81, 82, 83, 85, 86, 87
No Credit: Items 84, 99–105

13-Month Item Set—Motor Scale
Credit: Items 61, 70
No Credit   Items 62–69

DON'T FORGET

7.3 Information to Include in the Background Section of a Report

Medical History

1. Relevant prenatal history (e.g., maternal substance use)
2. Birth history—gestational age, birth weight, complications
3. Early growth and developmental history
4. Medical concerns, disabilities, etc.
5. Hospitalizations, chronic and concurrent illnesses

Social History

1. Family constellation—who lives in the home
2. Ages of siblings, parents
3. Employment status of parents
4. Day care or alternative caregivers
5. Financial status (recipient of public assistance, including food stamps, WIC)
6. History of abuse or neglect—involvement with foster care or child protective services
7. Involvement with other social agencies—family support programs, church

Developmental History

1. Feeding
2. Sleeping
3. Language—comprehension and expression
4. Playing
5. Toileting
6. Social interactions
7. Response to change in routine
8. Prior evaluations
9. Intervention or involvement with other programs

Because she did not achieve basal on the 13-month motor item set, the 12-month item set was administered. It consisted of three additional items and was scored as follows:

12-Month Item Set—Motor Scale

Credit: Items, 58, 59, 60

On the Mental Scale Karla achieved a basal in the 13-month item set because she received credit for at least five items. She also achieved a ceiling in the 13-month item set because she did not receive credit for at least three items. The highest item in the item set preceding the item set where she established basal is 77. Therefore her raw score is 86 (77 + 9 [she received credit for 9 items]).

On the Motor Scale Karla did not achieve a basal in the 13-month item set because she did not receive credit for at least four items. Therefore the 12-month item set was administered (three additional items). Karla received credit for the three additional items. Therefore she achieved a basal in the 12-month item set. She achieved a ceiling in the 13-month item set because she did not receive credit for at least two items. The highest item in the item set preceding the item set where she achieved a basal is 57. Karla's raw score for the Motor Scale is 62 (57 + 5 [she received credit for 5 items]).

To determine Karla's MDI and PDI, the norm tables for 13-month-old children was used because Karla is between 12 months, 16 days, and 13 months, 15 days (Table A.1., p. 268, of the BSID-II manual). She obtained an MDI of 89 and a PDI of 82.

Her MDI is classified as Within Normal Limits (within 1 standard deviation from the mean). With an MDI of 89, Karla's mental skills are between the 16th and 25th percentile, meaning that her scores are better than 16% to 25% of the 13-month-old infants in the standardization sample (Table 7.1, p. 228, of the BSID-II manual). Based on a mental raw score of 86, Karla's mental developmental age is 11 months (Table B.2, p. 325, of the BSID-II manual). Karla's mental performance is a typical pattern. She received credit for all items through Item 83, had intermittent credits and no credits through Item 87, and received no credit for all items beyond Item 87. The items in which she was successful tapped a range of skills, including receptive and expressive language, perceptual-motor integration, and imitation (cognitive).

Karla's PDI is classified as Mildly Delayed Performance (greater than 1 standard deviation below the mean). An index score of 82 is between the 9th

DON'T FORGET

7.4 Information to Include in Appearance and Behavioral Observations

Appearance

1. Size—height and weight
2. Grooming—cleanliness
3. Appropriateness of clothes
4. Any unusual physical characteristics
5. Alert or signs of fatigue
6. Signs of illness (coughing, runny nose)
7. Also include appearance of caregiver, if notable

Infant's Behavior (in comparison with expectations for chronological age)

1. Interaction with examiner—eye contact, responsivity
2. Affect—smiling, whining
3. Cooperation or resistance
4. Activity—fidgets, sits in chair
5. Attention span and level of distractibility
6. Language—spontaneous, response to examiner
7. Interest in test materials or in completing tasks
8. Process used to solve problems—imitation, trial and error, help seeking
9. Frustration tolerance

Infant's Interaction With Caregiver

1. Approach to caregiver
2. Looks to caregiver for assistance or when in distress
3. Looks to caregiver for acknowledgment of success

Caregiver's Interaction With Infant

1. Approach to infant
2. Supportive—encourages infant
3. Intrusive—does task for infant
4. Hostile—negative comments or actions toward infant

Validity of Assessment

1. Include caregiver's appraisal (first two questions on BRS) regarding how typical infant's behavior was and whether the infant could have done better.
2. Does the test represent a valid assessment of infant's skills—why or why not?
3. If it was not a valid assessment, indicate what would be necessary for the assessment to be valid.

and 16th percentile (Table 7.1, p. 228, of the BSID-II manual). In other words, between 84% and 91% of the 13-month-old children in the standardization sample had higher scores on the PDI than Karla did. Based on a motor raw score of 62, Karla's motor developmental age is 11 months (Table B.2, p. 325, of the BSID-II manual). Looking at the pattern of Karla's motor performance, she is able to stand alone (Item 61) and walk with help (Item 60), but not walk alone (Item 62). Motor Quality on the BRS was rated as Within Normal Limits. Thus there does not appear to be any abnormality in the quality of her motor movement, such as poor tone, pacing, or coordination, although her gross motor ability was not always appropriate for the demands of the tasks for her age.

It may seem confusing that Karla's mental and motor developmental age are both at the 11-month level, even though her MDI is classified Within Normal Limits and her PDI is classified Mildly Delayed Performance. There are several possible explanations. First, the confidence intervals indicate that there is 90% likelihood that her true MDI is between 83 and 99 and her true PDI is between 77 and 93, indicating a great deal of overlap. Second, Karla's MDI of 89 is only 7 points higher than her PDI of 82. This discrepancy is not significant and is relatively common (52.5% of the children in the standardization sample had an MDI > PDI difference of at least 9). Third, Karla's MDI of 89 is near the upper range of the Mildly Delayed Performance classification. Finally, on the developmental age tables, Karla's mental raw score is at the top of the 11-month developmental age category and her motor raw score is in the middle of the 11-month developmental age category.

Recommendations

Although Karla may not meet criteria for referral for early intervention based on her developmental scores or her behavior during testing, there are at least five significant risk factors that may interfere with her healthy development. First, she is the daughter of an adolescent mother who is not in school, not working, and not in a relationship with the baby's father. Children of adolescent parents are at significant risk for developmental problems, particularly in the context of other social problems (Furstenberg, Brooks-Gunn, & Morgan, 1987). Second, Karla's growth has fallen off and she has experienced a decel-

DON'T FORGET

7.5 Information to Include in Results

Test Environment—Adaptation

1. Indicate where test was administered (office, home, hospital room).
2. Indicate any changes in standard administration procedures.
3. Indicate if test was administered over two sessions or if session had to be interrupted.

Results

1. Report results (percentile scores and classification from BRS, MDI and PDI from Mental and Motor Scales), but write in language that can be understood by someone unfamiliar with the BSID-II.
2. Include developmental ages if they are helpful in interpretation.
3. Summarize the infant's strengths and weaknesses by looking for performance patterns; identify emerging skills.
4. Do not list every item indicating whether credit was or was not received; focus on underlying abilities.
5. Indicate how child's behavior may have influenced test performance.
6. Relate results to previous evaluations or to other tests and provide explanations for inconsistencies (e.g., restandardization of Bayley Scales if there is a BSID–BSID-II discrepancy).

eration in both her weight and height. Children with early failure to thrive are at risk for long-term developmental problems (Oates, Peacock, & Forrest, 1984). Third, Karla's mother and grandmother report that there is tension in the home around feeding. Karla frequently refuses to eat and her mother tries to force-feed her. Fourth, although the interaction between Karla and her grandmother appears to be warm and nurturant, the relationship between Karla and her mother and between Karla's mother and her own mother appears to be strained. Family stress can have a negative impact on children's development (Crnic, Ragozin, Greenberg, Robinson, and Basham, 1983). Finally, this is a low-income family with few economic resources and few supports. Poverty and lack of social support can interfere with healthy parenting and with healthy child development (McLoyd, 1990).

It might be most useful to tell Karla's mother and grandmother that her skills are closer to a child of 11 months than to a child of 13 months and to give them specific recommendations for activities that would enhance her developmental skills. For example, she enjoyed the task of releasing cubes into a cup and placing one peg into a peg board, but she was not successful with form boards. Manipulation tasks, such as simple puzzles or shape sorters may enable her to practice and extend her skills. It may also be useful for Karla to be encouraged to pull to standing and to cruise along furniture to practice her motor skills of standing and walking. Karla's developmental progress should be monitored to ensure that she gains skills at an adequate rate.

The administration of the BSID-II revealed serious problems in Karla's relationship with her mother. Karla's poor growth appears to be the result of a lack of calories, related to the quality of her interaction with her mother. In addition, Karla appears to have developed a closer relationship with her grandmother than with her mother, a relatively common occurrence among children of adolescent mothers. Thus there are serious threats to Karla's development. Karla and her mother should be referred to an intervention program that focuses on parent-infant interactions, particularly regarding feeding. A nutritionist might also be consulted. In addition, Karla's mother should be referred to mental health services to improve her relationship with her mother and daughter.

Case 2: Jacob L.

	Score	Category
BRS	45th percentile	Within Normal Limits
MDI	89	Within Normal Limits
PDI	94	Within Normal Limits

Reason for Referral

Jacob is a 20-month-old infant who was referred for evaluation by his pediatrician because he is not talking. The referral question is to evaluate Jacob's development to determine if he is eligible for early intervention services.

DON'T FORGET

7.6 Information to Include in Summary and Recommendations

- Use results from BSID-II and other assessments to address questions raised by referral source.
- Summarize findings mentioned earlier in report—do not introduce new findings.
- Summarize outstanding or additional questions or areas to be addressed.
- Develop recommendations for a treatment plan.
- Include recommendations for anticipatory guidance (activities caregivers can do at home) based on infant's behavior and test performance.
- Indicate whether recommendations have been discussed with caregivers.
- Include recommendations for referrals. Indicate if and when follow-up is recommended.
- Be as specific as possible (e.g., names and phone numbers of possible referral sources, if appropriate and available).

Background

Jacob was born at 34 weeks gestation. His birth weight and length were appropriate for his gestational age and he had no complications. After a 3-week hospital stay, he was discharged to the care of his parents. Jacob grew well and appeared to have no medical problems resulting from his early birth. He had four episodes of otitis media in the 1st year of life. Since his first birthday, he has had only one episode of otitis media. He has had no hospitalizations since birth.

Jacob lives with his biological parents and 4-year-old sister. His parents are college educated and both work full time in the software industry. Jacob attends family day care in his middle-class neighborhood in a home with four other preschool-aged children.

The notes from Jacob's pediatrician indicate that his early development was within normal limits when corrected for prematurity. He was followed closely and his parents were compliant with appointments and recommendations. Jacob adjusted well to his family's routine and besides the frequent episodes of otitis media, there have been no medical concerns. Jacob's parents expressed their concern about his limited vocabulary (approximately 10 single words). They also noted that he is sometimes moody and has frequent fights with his older sister.

Appearance and Behavioral Observation

Jacob presented as a well-groomed, neatly dressed toddler. He was accompanied by both parents, and he separated immediately from them to approach the toys in the room. There was little spontaneous vocalization as he played alone, but there was occasional babbling when Jacob approached his parents.

During testing, Jacob sat at a child-sized table and chairs. His attention and cooperation varied by the demands of the tasks. On visual-motor tasks, his attention was very focused and he was clearly pleased when he successfully completed a task. However, during verbal tasks, his attention waned and he was easily distracted. In addition, transitions were often difficult as he protested by holding on to items when the examiner tried to replace one item with another.

Jacob's parents reported that his behavior during testing was typical to his behavior at home and that his performance was excellent. Based on his behavior and his parent's report, the testing was assumed to be a valid representation of Jacob's skills.

Results

Jacob was born at 34 weeks and his chronological age was 20 months, 18 days. His chronological age was corrected for prematurity by subtracting 6 weeks, resulting in a corrected age of 19 months, 6 days. Testing was begun using the 17- to 19-month item set.

On the BRS, Jacob obtained an overall score at the 45th percentile, which is Within Normal Limits. On Orientation/Engagement, Emotional Regulation, and Motor Quality he obtained scores at the 35th, 55th, and 75th percentiles, all Within Normal Limits.

The 17- to 19-month item set was administered for the Mental and Motor Scales and was scored as follows:

17- to 19-Month Item Set—Mental Scale
Credit: Items 97, 98, 100–105, 108, 115, 116, 119, 120, 123
No Credit: Items 99, 106, 107, 109, 110, 111, 113, 114, 117, 118, 121,
                 122, 124–126

17- to 19-Month Item Set—Motor Scale
Credit: Items 66–72, 74, 75, 76
No Credit: Items 73, 77–82

On the Mental Scale Jacob achieved the basal and ceiling in the 17- to 19-month item set because he received credit for at least five items and no credit for at least three items. The highest item in the item set preceding the 17- to 19-month item set is 96. Therefore his raw score is 111 (96 + 15 [he received credit for 15 items]).

Using Jacob's corrected age of 19 months, 6 days, and the Norms Tables for children from 18 months, 16 days, to 19 months, 15 days (Table A.1, pp. 280–281 of the BSID-II manual), he obtained an MDI of 89, which is classified Within Normal Limits. Using the Developmental Age Table (Table B.2, p. 325, of the BSID-II manual), Jacob's raw score of 111 translates to a mental developmental age of 17 months. Looking at the item level of his performance on the MDI indicates that he had much more difficulty with verbal items than with perceptual motor items.

Facet scores were determined because Jacob's performance was uneven. Jacob received credit on the Cognitive facet for items through 18 months, with success on two of five items at 19 months. Thus, according to the Cognitive facet, his developmental age equivalent is 18 months. However, on the Language facet, his performance was uneven. He was unsuccessful on the one 11-month language item, demonstrated success on both 12-month items, and received credit for only 1 of 12 items that tap skills between the 13th and 18th month. Jacob's developmental age equivalent for language is considered to be 12 months. Based on developmental age at the facet level and item-level information, Jacob demonstrates a receptive and expressive language delay, relative to his cognitive skills.

In Jacob's case, correcting for prematurity and not examining the pattern of his responses could result in a false interpretation that his development is Within Normal Limits. However, there are at least four pieces of evidence that suggest that Jacob is experiencing a language delay. First, his parents expressed their concern about his limited vocabulary. Second, during the evaluation Jacob spoke no words, made only a few sounds, and could not reliably follow verbal directions. Third, Jacob's behavior differed as a function of the items that were administered. During administration of verbal items he was distractible and less attentive. In contrast, during administration of visual-motor tasks, he was very cooperative and attentive. Children's behavior frequently disintegrates when they are confronted with tasks that are above their skill level or that they perceive as difficult. Finally, the discrepancy between the Cognitive and Language facet scores points to a language delay. The examiner may test the limits of Jacob's language skills by administering language items below the basal that Jacob established on the Mental Scale. Jacob's performance on these items would not alter his MDI but would provide useful descriptive information on his language skills that should be presented in a report. Thus the MDI provides only a partial picture of Jacob's mental skills, whether it is corrected for prematurity or not.

On the Motor Scale Jacob received a basal and ceiling in the 17- to 19-month item set because he received credit for at least four items and no credit for at least two items. The highest item in the item set preceding the 17- to 19-month item set is 65. Therefore his raw score is 75 (65 + 10 [he received credit for 10 items]).

Using Jacob's corrected age of 19 months, 6 days, and the Norms Tables for children from 18 months, 16 days, to 19 months, 15 days (Table A.1, pp. 280–281 of the BSID-II manual), he obtained a PDI of 94, which is rated Within Normal Limits. Using the Developmental Age Table (Table B.2, p. 325, of the BSID-II manual), Jacob's raw score of 75 translates to a motor developmental age equivalent of 17 months.

The pattern of Jacob's motor skills is consistent with developmental expectations—a series of credits, credits and no credits, and finally a series of no credits. He could walk forward and backward, stand on either foot with help, but he could not run, jump, or ascend or descend steps independently.

Recommendations

Jacob's parents should be told that Jacob's language skills are delayed, as they recognized. However, his cognitive skills and motor skills are developing well. Jacob should be referred for a hearing test and a thorough language evalua-

ILLUSTRATIVE CASE REPORTS 137

tion, with intervention as indicated. Feedback to Jacob's parents should include a discussion regarding his behavior. The moodiness and sibling fights they mentioned may be partially related to his frustration regarding his limited language skills. His cooperation and attentiveness during the administration of the visual-motor items on the BSID-II illustrate his enjoyment with those types of activities and his ability to comply and attend. Intervention following the hearing and language evaluations may alleviate Jacob's mild behavioral problems, as Jacob's language skills improve.

Case 3: George K.

	Score	Category
BRS	65th percentile	Within Normal Limits
MDI	88	Within Normal Limits
PDI	116	Accelerated Performance

Reason for Referral

George is a 36-month-old child who is enrolled in a federally funded study of children born to substance-abusing women. He has been enrolled in the study since birth and was evaluated on the BSID at 6 and 12 months and on the BSID-II at 24 months. This will be George's final evaluation.

Background

George was born at 37 weeks to a 28-year-old woman with chronic schizophrenia who admitted using cocaine and heroin throughout her pregnancy. George's birth weight of 2,000 grams (4 pounds, 7 ounces) was small for gestational age, but his length of 48.4 centimeters (19 inches) was appropriate for gestational age. He had Neonatal Abstinence syndrome at delivery (physiological distress associated with drug withdrawal) and remained in the hospital for 3 weeks. Following discharge, George grew well and by 6 months of age his growth was Within Normal Limits. He has had no hospitalizations, no illnesses beyond mild upper respiratory infections, and no injuries. His immunizations are up to date.

George was discharged from the hospital into his mother's care and lived with his mother and great grandmother. His mother was participating in a research project that provides drug treatment, rehabilitation, and vocational training for her and center-based day care and primary care for George. Initially George's mother had trouble with compliance, but after one referral to child protective services, her compliance improved and she and George attend the program almost daily. George's mother claims that she has been drug free since George's birth. The family is financially supported through SSI that George's mother obtains due to her mental health disability. George's father is unknown.

Appearance and Behavioral Observation

George was accompanied by his mother. He was clean and appropriately dressed. Initially George sat beside his mother with his head down and had difficulty making eye contact with the examiner. However, after a brief warm-up period, he expressed interest in the toys and joined the examiner at the child-sized table and chairs. He was cooperative during the session, but when he had difficulty with an item, he gave up quickly and averted his eyes. He rarely smiled and only spoke when the examiner asked a direct question.

George's mother sat quietly during the evaluation. She answered questions when asked but did not volunteer information. George did not look to her and she did not offer encouragement to him. When the session ended, they walked off together without saying a word to one another.

When asked if George's behavior was typical and if he did as well as expected, George's mother nodded in agreement but did not elaborate. George's behavior and the pattern of responses suggest that the BSID-II was a valid representation of his skills.

Results

On the BRS George obtained an overall score at the 65th percentile, which is Within Normal Limits. In Orientation/Engagement, Emotional Regulation, and Motor Quality, he obtained scores at the 70th, 45th, and 90th percentiles, respectively. All scores are Within Normal Limits.

The 35- to 37-month item set was administered for the Mental and Motor Scales and was scored as follows:

35- to 37-Month Item Set—Mental Scale
Credit: Items 140–146, 149, 150, 151, 154
No Credit: Items 147, 148, 152, 153, 155, 156–161, 163–168

35- to 37-Month Item Set—Motor Scale
Credit: Items 91–100, 102, 103, 106, 109
No Credit: Items 101, 104, 105, 107, 108, 110, 111

On the Mental Scale, George established a basal and a ceiling within the 35- to 37-month item set because he received credit for at least five items and no credit for at least three items. The highest item in the item set preceding the 35- to 37-month items set is 139. Therefore his raw score is 149 (139 + 10 [he received credit for 10 items]).

Using George's age of 36 months, 10 days, and the Norms Tables for children from 35 months, 16 days, to 36 months, 15 days (Table A.1, pp. 314–315 of the BSID-II manual), he obtained an MDI of 88, which is classified Within Normal Limits. Using the Developmental Age Table (Table B.2, p. 325, of the BSID-II manual), George's raw score of 149 translates to a mental developmental age of 32 months.

George's performance at the item level suggests that his cognitive development is proceeding evenly across language acquisition, knowledge of early concepts, visual-motor integration, and problem solving. On the Motor Scale George established a basal within the 35- to 37-month item set because he received credit for at least four items. A ceiling was also established because he received no credit for at least two items. The highest item in the item set preceding the 35- to 37-month items set is 90. Therefore his raw score is 104 (90 + 14 [he received credit for 14 items]).

Using George's age of 36 months, 10 days, and the Norms Tables for children from 35 months, 16 days, to 36 months, 15 days (Table A.1, pp. 314–315 of the BSID-II manual), he obtained a PDI of 116, which is classified Accelerated Performance. Using the Developmental Age Table (Table B.2, p. 325, of the BSID-II manual), George's raw score of 104 translates to a motor developmental age of 40 to 42 months.

George achieved a PDI score that was above the 84th percentile and therefore higher than 84% of the 36-month-old children in the standardization sample (see Table 7.2, p. 228, in the BSID-II manual). Inspection of George's item-level performance on the Motor Scale indicates that although his motor skills are above normal, his gross motor skills (e.g., ascending and descending steps, running, and jumping) are slightly better developed than his fine motor skills (e.g., buttoning, copying and tracing designs).

George's MDI of 88 is 28 points below his PDI of 116. This discrepancy is statistically significant (Table 5.8, p. 198, of the BSID-II manual). In the standardization sample, 10% of the children obtained PDI scores that were at least 28 points higher than their MDI scores. Although such a difference is relatively rare, because George's MDI and PDI scores are both rated Within Normal Limits, there is little concern at this time.

This is the fourth time that George has been evaluated on the Bayley Scales. At 6 months, his MDI was 110 and his PDI was 108. At 12 months, his MDI was 114 and his PDI was 120, indicating relative stability over the 1st year of life. When he was evaluated at 24 months his MDI was 90 and his PDI was 110. The examiner attributed the drop in George's MDI to the change in test. The BSID-II was administered at 24 months, rather than the BSID, which had been administered at 6 and 12 months. (There is approximately a 10-point difference in scores between the BSID and the BSID-II.) George's performance on the Infant Behavior Record at 6 and 12 months and on the BRS at 24 and 36 months is consistent. Examiners have commented that he is a quiet child, who is "slow to warm up." However, he is compliant, cooperative, and works hard.

George's performance at 36 months suggests that he has experienced similar growth in both mental and motor skills over the past year because his MDI and PDI have been relatively consistent. This is a significant finding because George has not demonstrated the drop in MDI scores that are frequently reported during the preschool years among children from low-income families (Burchinal et al., 1997).

Recommendations

Despite his prenatal exposure to cocaine and heroin, George has continuously demonstrated cognitive development within the normal range and motor development above the normal range. Feedback to George's mother should emphasize how well he is developing, with the goal of helping her feel pride in her son and in her role as his mother. Although it is likely that George has benefited from the center-based day care experience that he has had since birth, he also spends many hours each day in the care of his mother and great grandmother.

As the research project ends, it would be beneficial for George to continue to participate in day care, perhaps through Head Start. In addition, George's mother should be encouraged to participate in parenting classes or activities through Head Start so that she is aware of the activities to expect from George and how to encourage him at home. Given the high-risk status of this family, George's development should continue to be monitored.

Case 4: Lydia M.

	Score	*Category*
BRS	35th percentile	Within Normal Limits
MDI	<50	Significantly Delayed Performance
PDI	<50	Significantly Delayed Performance

Reason for Referral

Lydia is 16 months of age. She was referred for an evaluation by her primary pediatrician to document her developmental status following placement of a ventriculoperitoneal shunt to relieve intracranial pressure. Lydia's parents have noted a decrease in her responsiveness.

Background

Lydia was born at 39 weeks gestation. Her birth weight and length were appropriate for gestational age and she was discharged after two days. She experienced Group B strep meningitis approximately 1 week after birth, followed by multiple neurological problems, including a seizure disorder, severe visual impairment, cerebral palsy, and profound mental retardation. Other than her neurological problems, she has not experienced health problems.

Lydia lives with her biological parents, who are 25 years of age and high school graduates. Lydia is their only child. Lydia's father works in construction and her mother is a homemaker. They have extended family nearby and participate in a support group for parents of children with special needs. Lydia receives SSI and WIC.

Lydia's mother described Lydia as a very calm baby who rarely cries. She has adjusted well to daily routines and sleeps through the night, with a 3-hour afternoon nap. She enjoys eating and her growth is Within Normal Limits. Lydia drinks from a bottle and eats pureed foods fed from a spoon.

Lydia received home-based early intervention for the 1st year of life and is now enrolled in a school for children with special needs. In addition to educational services, she receives physical therapy, occupational therapy, and speech therapy. Therapists have worked with Lydia's parents on positioning, feeding, and developmental activities.

Appearance and Behavioral Observations

Lydia was very clean and neatly dressed. She was seated in a therapeutic wheelchair that provided head and trunk support with her hands flexed and her arms in a retracted position. At least three times during the evaluation Lydia had seizures in which her eyes rolled back and she had spasms in her upper body. She recovered quickly without any apparent change in behavior. Lydia made guttural sounds and appeared to smile on several occasions.

Lydia was accompanied by her mother, who was very attractive and an excellent historian. She had a notebook that included pertinent information about Lydia's medical history, together with copies of evaluations and recommendations. Several times during the evaluation, she patted Lydia or placed her arm on Lydia's shoulder in a comforting manner.

Most of the items on the Mental Scale were administered using a lapboard with Lydia sitting in her therapeutic wheelchair to ensure that she had adequate head and trunk support. The Motor Scale was administered on a mat on the floor. Lydia was quiet and did not protest when she was placed in various positions. She did not respond to verbal instructions and could not follow visual cues because she has a severe visual impairment. Although Lydia's mother said she thought the child could detect movement, there was no evidence that she could visually track objects or the examiner.

Lydia's mother reported that her behavior during testing was typical of her behavior in other settings. She also indicated that the developmental skills that

Lydia demonstrated, albeit minimal, were consistent with the skills she demonstrated at school and home, and therefore were representative.

Results

Given the severity of Lydia's developmental disabilities, it was necessary to estimate the appropriate item sets for the Mental and Motor Scale and to adapt the administrative procedures.

To determine which Mental Scale item set to use, Lydia was given a cube while she was seated in her therapeutic chair. She held the cube and brought it to her mouth but did not try to locate it when it dropped. She did not reach for the ring. Given the information available about Lydia's speech and vision, as well as her motor impairment and her performance on a few items, the 3-month item set was administered for the Mental Scale and was scored as follows:

3-Month Item Set—Mental Scale

Credit: Items 21, 22, 30, 31, 35, 37, 40

No Credit: Items 20, 23–29, 32–34, 36, 38, 39

3-Month Item Set—Motor Scale

Credit: Items 11–21, 25, 26

No Credit: Items 22–24, 27, 28

Because Lydia's mental skills are hindered by her visual impairment, several items were administered with a slight alteration in instructions. This decision was made knowing that Lydia would not be able to perform the items without alterations. Auditory and tactile cues were substituted for visual cues when possible. For example when Items 38 and 39 (Reaches for Suspended Ring and Grasps Suspended Ring) were administered, the ring was placed in Lydia's hand while calling her name. The ring was then removed from her hand and placed in the lapboard and her hand was guided to the ring. However, she still made no attempt to pick up the ring independently. If the ring was placed in her hand, she could retain it and bring it to her mouth, but she could not reach and grasp. Her hands were usually maintained in a flexed (fisted) position.

On the Mental Scale Lydia achieved a basal in the 3-month item set because she received credit for at least five items. She also achieved a ceiling in the 3-month item set because she did not receive credit for at least three items.

Given the level of Lydia's disability, the examiner tested the limits of her ability by including items from the 2- and 4-month item sets. However, Lydia did not receive credit on any additional items. The highest item in the item set preceding the item set where she established basal is 19. Therefore her raw score is 26 (19 + 7 [she received credit for 7 items]).

To estimate the appropriate Motor Scale item set, Lydia was placed in a prone position on the mat. She was able to raise her head and trunk to 45 degrees, but she could not reliably support her head. Her mother reported that she could roll from her stomach to back but not from her back to her stomach. Therefore we estimated that her motor development should be evaluated within the 3-month item set.

On the Motor Scale, Lydia achieved a basal in the 3-month item set because she received credit for at least four items. She also achieved a ceiling in the 3-month item set because she did not receive credit for at least two items. The highest item in the item set preceding the item set where she established basal is 10. Lydia's raw score for the Motor Scale is 23 (10 + 13 [she received credit for 13 items]). Lydia's performance was hindered by her lack of control and her increased tone.

To determine Lydia's MDI and PDI, the Norm Tables for 26-month-old children were used because Lydia is between 25 months, 16 days, and 26 months, 15 days (Table A.1, pp. 294–95 of the BSID-II manual). Because both her MDI and PDI were below 50, she is classified as having Significantly Delayed Performance.

Based on a mental raw score of 26, Lydia's mental developmental age is 2 months (Table B-2, p. 325, of the BSID-II manual). Lydia's cognitive performance suggests an abnormal pattern because credit and no credit items are spread throughout the item set. Her neurological disabilities, particularly her visual impairment and her inability to reach and grasp are major impediments to her development. Lydia did seem to enjoy auditory and tactile stimulation.

Based on a motor raw score of 23, Lydia's motor developmental age equivalent is 3 months (Table B-2, p. 325, of the BSID-II manual). The pattern of her responses indicates a relatively consistent pattern of credits, followed by a mixture of credits and no credits, and then no credits. Again, Lydia's neurological disabilities, particularly her increased tone, interfere with her motor development. The extrapolated developmental index scores developed by Robinson and Mervis (1996) could not be used because Lydia's estimated developmental indices are below 30, and therefore not on the table.

Given Lydia's level of disability, her scores on the BRS have to be interpreted with caution because her behavior is not consistent with the behavior of a 16-month-old infant. Lydia was attentive and cooperative. Her overall score was at the 35th percentile and she achieved scores that were rated Within Normal Limits for Emotional Regulation and Orientation/Engagement. Her Motor Quality was rated in the Non-Optimal range, reflecting her increased tone and seizures.

Recommendations

Lydia has a severe developmental disability. Her cognitive skills are at a 2-month level and her motor skills are at a 3-month level. Since she seems to enjoy auditory and tactile stimulation, activities that involve those senses are recommended. For example, Lydia's parents should talk to her during daily activities and provide tactile support, as her mother did during the evaluation. Given her increased tone, she may also benefit from relaxation activities. Lydia attends school daily where she receives physical, occupational, and speech therapy and developmental stimulation.

Lydia has adjusted well to her family's routine, with no problems in feeding or sleeping. It is apparent that Lydia's parents see her as a "special" child and treat her with care and affection. In addition, their involvement with extended family and a parent group provides them with support.

SUMMARY

When reporting results from the Bayley Scales, it is important to keep in mind the purpose of testing. While the MDI and PDI are the most psychometrically sound scores, the examiner's ability to interpret the pattern of an infant's performance is equally important in formulating recommendations and directing the infant to the services needed.

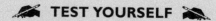

TEST YOURSELF

1. **Examiners often administer multiple tests, depending on the referral question and the infant's level of functioning. Because the BSID-II has been revised with recent norms, examiners should**

    (a) not report scores from other tests because the scores are likely to differ and may confuse the reader.

    (b) report scores from other tests but also include a theoretical discussion of norms so that readers understand why test scores may differ.

    (c) report other scores with a brief discussion of differences in norms.

    (d) not report other scores because the BSID-II is a comprehensive, psychometrically sound test.

2. **Which of the following should not be included in a report?**

    (a) the question to be addressed by the report

    (b) scores from previous tests

    (c) social history abut the infant's family

    (d) relative's commentary about the family

3. **It is not necessary to report MDI and PDI scores if you have reported developmental age.** True or False?

4. **The Behavior and Appearance sections of a report should include**

    (a) a summary of the results.

    (b) a statement about the validity of the test.

    (c) the referral question.

    (d) a summary of the recommendations.

5. **Most of the time, it is not necessary to report more than the MDI and PDI scores.** True or False?

6. **It is beneficial to list all the items administered and whether the infant did or did not receive credit.** True or False?

7. **Reports cannot be read by parents.** True or False?

Answers: 1. c; 2. d; 3. False; 4. b; 5. False; 6. False; 7. False

References

Aggarwal, P., Chaudhari, S., Bhave, S., Pandit, A., & Barve, S. (1998). Clinical predictors of outcome in hypoxic ischaemic encephalopathy in term infants. *Annals of Tropical Paediatrics, 18,* 117–121.

Als, H. (1997). Earliest intervention for preterm infants in the Newborn Intensive Care Unit. In M. J. Guralnick (Ed)., *The effectiveness of early intervention* (pp. 47–76). Baltimore: Brookes.

American Psychological Association. (1985). *Standards for educational and psychological testing.* San Antonio, TX: Author.

Arendt, R., Singer, L., Angelopoulos, J., Bass-Busdiecker, O., & Mascia, J. M. (1998). Sensorimotor development in cocaine-exposed infants. *Infant Behavior & Development, 21,* 627–640.

Aylward, G. P. (1992). The relationship between environmental risk and developmental outcome. *Journal of Developmental and Behavioral Pediatrics, 13,* 222–229.

Aylward, G. P. (1994). *Practitioner's guide to developmental and psychological testing.* New York: Plenum Press.

Aylward, G. P. (1995). *Bayley Infant Neurological Screener.* San Antonio: Psychological Corporation.

Aylward, G. P. (1997). *Infant and early childhood neuropsychology.* New York: Plenum Press.

Aylward, G. P., & Kenny, T. J. (1979). Developmental follow-up: Inherent problems and a conceptual model. *Journal of Pediatric Psychology, 4,* 331–343.

Aylward, G. P., Peiffer, S. I., Wright, A., & Verhulst, S. J. (1989). Outcome studies of low birth weight infants published in the last decade: A metaanalysis. *Journal of Pediatrics, 115,* 515–520.

Aylward, G. P., Verhulst, S. J., Bell, S., & Gyurke, J. S. (1995). Cognitive and motor score differences in biologically at-risk infants. *Infant Behavior and Development, 18,* 43–52.

Bayley, N. (1933). *The California First-Year Mental Scale.* Berkeley: University of California Press.

Bayley, N. (1936). *The California Infant Scale of Motor Development.* Berkeley: University of California Press.

Bayley, N. (1969). *Manual for the Bayley Scales of Infant Development.* San Antonio, TX: Psychological Corporation.

Bayley, N. (1993). *Manual for the Bayley Scales of Infant Development* (2nd ed.). San Antonio, TX: Psychological Corporation.

Bayley, N., & Schaefer, E. S. (1964). Correlations of maternal and child behaviors with the development of mental abilities. Data from the Berkeley Growth Study. *Monographs of the Society for Research in Child Development, 29* (6, Serial No. 97).

Bellinger, D. C., Jonas, R. A., Rappaport, L. A., Wypij, D., Wernovsky, G., Kubar, K. C. K., Barnes, P. D., Holmes, G. L., Hickey, P. R., Strand, R. D., Walsh, A. Z., Helmens, S. L., Constantizou, J. E., Carrazara, E. J., Mayer, J. E., Hanley, F. L., Castaneda,

A. R., Ware, J. H., & Newburger, J. W. (1995). Developmental and neurologic status of children after heart surgery with hypothermic cirulatory arrest or low-flow cardiopulmonary bypass. *New England Journal of Medicine, 332*, 549–555.

Belsky, J. (1984). The determinants of parenting: A process model. *Child Development, 55*, 83–96.

Black, M. M. (1991). Early intervention services for infants and toddlers: A focus on families. *Journal of Clinical Child Psychology, 20*, 51–57.

Black, M. M., Dubowitz, H., Hutcheson, J., Berenson-Howard, J., & Starr, R. H. (1995). A randomized clinical trial of home intervention among families of children with failure to thrive. *Pediatrics, 95*, 807–814.

Black, M. M., Schuler, M., & Nair, P. (1993). Prenatal drug exposure: Neurodevelopmental outcome and parenting environment. *Journal of Pediatric Psychology, 18*, 605–620.

Bradley, R. H., Whiteside, L., Mundfrom, D. J., Casey, P. H., Kelleher, K. J., & Pope, S. K. (1994). Early indications of resilience and their relation to experiences in the home environment of low birth weight, premature children living in poverty. *Child Development, 65*, 346–360.

Brazelton, T. B. (1973). *Neonatal Behavioral Assessment Scale*. Philadelphia: Lippincott.

Brazelton, T. B. (1984). *Neonatal Behavioral Assessment Scale* (2nd ed.). Philadelphia: Lippincott.

Brazelton, T. B., & Nugent, J. K. (1995). *Neonatal Behavioral Assessment Scale* (3rd ed.). Cambridge, MA: Cambridge University Press.

Bronfenbrenner, U. (1979). *The ecology of human development—Experiments by nature and design*. Cambridge, MA: Harvard University Press.

Bronfenbrenner, U. (1993). Ecological systems theory. In R. Wozniak & K. Fisher (Eds.), *Specific environments: Thinking in contexts* (pp. 3–44). Hillsdale, NJ: Erlbaum.

Brooks-Gunn, J., & Duncan, G. (1997). The effects of poverty on children. *The Future of Children, 7*, 55–71.

Bruininks, R. H., Woodcock, R. W., Weatherman, R. F., & Hill, B. K. (1984). *Scales of Independent Behavior*. Allen, TX: DLM Teaching Resources.

Burchinal, M. R., Campbell, F. A., Bryant, D. M., Wasik, B. H., & Ramey, C. T. (1997). Early intervention and mediating processes in cognitive performance of children of low-income African-American families. *Child Development, 68*, 935–954.

Burns, W. J., Burns, K. A., & Kabacoff, R. I. (1992). Item and factor analyses of the Bayley Scales of Infant Development. *Advances in Infancy Research, 7*, 199–214.

Bzoch, K. R., & League, R. (1970). *Receptive-Expressive Emergent Language Scale*. Baltimore: University Park Press.

Cairns, R. B. (1983). The emergence of developmental psychology, in Musser, R. *Handbook of child psychology*, 4th ed., vol. 1. New York: Wiley.

Campbell, S. K., Siegel, E., Parr, C. A., & Ramey, C. T. (1986). Evidence for the need to renorm the Bayley Scales of Infant Development based on the performance of a population-based sample of 12-month-old infants. *Topics in Early Childhood Special Education, 6*, 83–96.

Capute, A., J., & Accardo, P. J. (1996a). The infant neurodevelopmental assessment: A clinical interpretative manual for CAT-CLAMS in the first two years of life, part 1. *Current Problems in Pediatrics, 26*, 238–257.

Capute, A., J., & Accardo, P. J. (1996b). The infant neurodevelopmental assessment: A clinical interpretative manual for CAT-CLAMS in the first two years of life, part 2. *Current Problems in Pediatrics, 26,* 279–306.

Cattell, P. (1940). *Cattell Infant Intelligence Scale.* San Antonio, TX: Psychological Corporation.

Chaudhari, S., Bhalerao, M. R., Vaidya, U., Pandit, A., & Nene, U. (1997). Growth and development of twins compared with singletons at ages one and four years. *Indian Pediatrics, 34,* 1081–1086.

Chung, M. J., Rhee, U. H., & Park, K. J. (1993). A preliminary study for the standardization of the Bayley Scales of Infant Development for Korean infants. *Korean Journal of Child Studies, 14,* 5–21.

Coie, J. D., Watt, N. F., West, S. G., Hawkins, J. D., Asarnow, J. R., Markman, H. J., Ramey, S. L., Shure, M. B., & Long, B. (1993). The science of prevention: A conceptual framework and some directions for a national research program. *American Psychologist, 48,* 1013–1022.

Cole, K. N., & Harris, S. R. (1992). Instability of the intelligence quotient-motor quotient relationship. *Developmental Medicine and Child Neurology, 34,* 633–641.

Coles, C. D., Platzman, K. A., Smith, I., James, M. E., & Falek, A. (1992). Effects of cocaine and alcohol use in pregnancy on neonatal growth and neuro-behavioral status. *Neurotoxicology and Teratology, 14,* 23–33.

Coplan, J. (1987). *Early Language Milestones Scale.* Austin, TX: Pre-ED Inc.

Costarides, A. H., & Shulman, B. B. (1998). Norm-referenced language measures: Implications for assessment of infants and toddlers. *Topics in Language Disorders, 18,* 26–33.

Crnic, K. A., Ragozin, A. S., Greenberg, M. T., Robinson, N. M., & Basham, R. B. (1983). Social interaction and developmental competence of preterm and full-term infants during the first year of life. *Child Development, 54,* 1199–1210.

DiLalla, L. F., Thompson, L. A., Plomin, R., Phillips, K., Fagan, J. F., Haith, M. M., Cyphers, L. H., & Fulker, D. W. (1990). Infant predictors of preschool and adult IQ: A study of infant twins and their parents. *Developmental Psychology, 26,* 759–769.

Drotar, D., Olness, K., Wiznitzer, M., Schatschneider, C., Marum, L., Guay, L., Fagan, J., Hom, D., Svilar. G., Ndugwa, C., & Mayengo, R. K. (1999). Neurodevelopmental outcomes of Ugandan infants with HIV infection: An application of growth curve analysis. *Health Psychology, 18,* 114–121.

Fagan, J. F., Singer, L. T., Montie, J. E., & Shepherd, P. A. (1986). Selective screening device for the early detection of normal or delayed cognitive development in infants at risk for later mental retardation. *Pediatrics, 78,* 1021–1026.

Fantz, R. L. & Fagan, J. F. (1975). Visual attention to size and number of pattern details by term and preterm infants during the first six months. *Child Development, 46,* 3–18.

Flynn, J. R. (1999). Searching for justice: The discovery of IQ gains over time. *American Psychologist, 54,* 5–20.

Frankenburg, W. K., & Dodds, J. B. (1967). The Denver Developmental Screening Test. *Journal of Pediatrics, 71,* 181–191.

Frankenburg, W. K., Dodds, J. B., Archer, P., & Bresnick, B. (1990). *Denver II Screening manual.* Denver: Denver Developmental Materials.

Frankenburg, W. K., Dodds, J. B., Archer, P., & Bresnick, B. (1992). The Denver II: A major revision and restandardization of the Denver Developmental Screening Test. *Pediatrics, 89,* 91–97.

Frankenburg, W. K., Fandal, A. W., Sciarillo, W., & Burgess, D. (1981). The newly abbreviated and revised Denver Developmental Screening Test. *Journal of Pediatrics, 99,* 995–999.

Frankenburg, W. K., Goldstein, A. D., & Camp, B. W. (1971). The revised Denver Developmental Screening Test: Its accuracy as a screening instrument. *Journal of Pediatrics, 79,* 988–995.

Furstenberg, F. F., Brooks-Gunn, J., & Morgan, S. (1987) *Adolescent mothers in later life.* Cambridge: Cambridge University Press.

Gauthier, S. M., Bauer, C. R., Messinger, D. S., & Closius, J. M. (1999). The Bayley Scales of Infant Development. II: Where to start? *Journal of Developmental and Behavioral Pediatrics, 20,* 75–79.

Gerken, K. C., Eliason, M. J., & Arthur, C. R. (1994). The assessment of at-risk infants and toddlers with the Bayley Mental Scale and the Battelle Developmental Inventory: Beyond the data. *Psychology in the Schools, 31,* 181–187.

Gesell, A. (1925). *The mental growth of the preschool child.* New York: Macmillan.

Gesell, A. (1948). *Studies in child development.* New York: Harper & Brothers.

Gesell, A., & Amatruda, C. (1941). *Developmental diagnosis.* New York: Paul B. Hoeber.

Glascoe, F. P., Bryne, K. E., Ashford, L. G., Johnson, K. L., Chang, B., & Strickland, B. (1992). Accuracy of the Denver-II in developmental screening. *Pediatrics, 89,* 1221–1225.

Godbole, K., Barve, S., & Chaudhari, S. (1997). Early predictors of neurodevelopmental outcome in high risk infants. *Indian Pediatrics, 34,* 491–495.

Goldstein, D. J., Fogle, E. E., Wieber, J. L., & O'Shea, T. M. (1995). Comparison of the Bayley Scales of Infant Development–Second Edition and the Bayley Scales of Infant Development with premature infants. *Journal of Psychoeducational Assessment, 13,* 391–396.

Griffiths, R. (1967). *The abilities of babies.* London: University of London Press.

Gunnar, M. R. (1998). Quality of early care and buffering of neuroendocrine stress reactions: Potential effects on the developing human brain. *Preventive Medicine: An International Journal Devoted to Practice and Theory, 27,* 208–211.

Guralnick, M. J. (1996). Second-generation research in the field of early intervention. In M. J. Guralnick (Ed.), *The effectiveness of early intervention* (pp. 3–22). Baltimore: Brookes.

Gyurke, J. S., & Aylward, G. P. (1992). Issues in the use of norm referenced assessments with at-risk infants. *The Child, Youth, and Family Services Quarterly, 15(3),* 6–9.

Hack, M., & Fanaroff, A. A. (1988). How small is too small? Considerations in evaluatng the outcome of the tiny infant. *Clinics in Perinatology, 15,* 773–788.

Hack, M., Taylor, H. G., Klein, N., Eiben, R., Schatschneider, C., & Mercuir-Minich, N. (1994). School-age outcomes in children with birth weights under 750 grams. *New England Journal of Medicine, 331,* 753–759.

Hart, T., & Risley, T. R. (1995). *Meaningful experiences in the everyday life of young American children.* Baltimore: Brookes.

Humphrey, J. H., Agoestina, T., Juliana, A., Septiana, S., Widjaja, H., Cerreto, M. C., Wu, L. S., Ichord, R. N., Katz, J., & West, K. P., Jr. (1998). Neonatal vitamin A supplementation: Effect on development and growth at 3 y of age. *American Journal of Clinical Nutrition, 68,* 109–17.

Hurt, H., Brodsky, N. L., Betancourt, L., & Braitman, L. E. (1995). Cocaine-exposed children: Follow-up through 30 months. *Journal of Developmental and Behavioral Pediatrics, 16,* 29–35.

Jaffa, A. S. (1934). *The California Preschool Mental Scale.* Berkeley, CA: University of California Press.

Kamphaus, R. W. (1993). *Clinical assessment of children's intelligence.* Boston: Allyn and Bacon.

Klerman, L. V. (1991). The health of poor children: Problems and programs. In A. C. Huston (Ed.), *Children in poverty* (pp. 136–157). Cambridge, England: Cambridge University Press.

Knolboch, H., Strauss, F., & Malone, A. E. (1980). *Manual of developmental diagnosis.* New York: Harper & Row.

Kopp, C. B., & McCall, R. B. (1982). Predicting later mental performance for normal, at-risk, and handicapped infants. *Life-span development and behavior* (pp. 33–61). New York: Academic Press.

Kraemer, H. C., Korner, A. F., & Hurwitz, S. (1985). A model for assessing the development of preterm infants as a function of gestational, conceptual, or chronological age. *Developmental Psychology, 21,* 806–812.

Kuhlman, F. A. (1922). *A handbook of mental tests.* New York: Wiley.

Leguire, L. E., Fellows, R. R., & Bier, G. (1990). Bayley Mental Scale of Infant Development and visually impaired children. *Journal of Visual Impairment and Blindness, 84,* 400–404.

LeTendre, D., Spiker, D., Scott, D. T., & Constantine, N. A. (1992). Establishing the "ceiling" on the Bayley Scales of Infant Development at 25 months. *Advances in Infancy Research, 7,* 187–198.

Lindsey, J. C., & Brouwers, P. (1999). Intrapolation and extrapolation of age-equivalent scores for the Bayley II: A comparison of two methods of estimation. *Clinical Neuropharmacology, 22,* 44–53.

Lozoff, B., Klein, N. K., Nelson, E. C., McClish, D. K., Manuel, M., & Chacon, M. E. (1998). Behavior of infants with iron-deficiency anemia. *Child Development, 69,* 24–36.

Lozoff, B., Wolf, A.W., & Jimenez, E. (1996). Iron-deficiency anemia and infant development: Effects of extended oral iron therapy. *Journal of Pediatrics,129,* 382–389.

Luster, T., & McAdoo, H. (1996). Family and child influences on educational attainment: A secondary analysis of the High/Scope Perry preschool data. *Developmental Psychology, 32,* 23–39.

Macias, M. M., Saylor, C. F., Greer, M. K., Charles, J. M., Bell, N., & Katikaneni, L. D. (1998). Infant screening: The usefulness of the Bayley Infant Neurodevelopmental Screener and the Clinical Adaptive Test/Clinical Linguistic Auditory Milestone Scale. *Journal of Developmental and Behavioral Pediatrics, 19,* 155–161.

Matheny, A. P. (1981). Bayley's Infant Behavior Record: Behavioral components and twin analyses. *Annual Progress in Child Psychiatry and Child Development,* 431–446.

Matheny, A. P. (1983). A longitudinal twin study of stability of components from Bayley's Infant Behavior Record. *Child Development, 54,* 356–360.

Matula, K., Gyurke, J. S., & Aylward, G. (1997). Response to commentary: Bayley Scales II. *Journal of Developmental and Behavioral Pediatrics, 18,* 112–113.

McCall, R. B. (1981). Nature-nurture and the two realms of development: A proposed integration with respect to mental development. *Child Development, 52,* 1–12.

McCarton, C. M., Brooks-Gunn, J., Wallace, I. F., Bauer, C. R., Bennett, F. C., Bernbaum, J. C., Broyles, R. S., Casey, P. H., McCormick, M. C., Scott, D. T., Tyson, J., Tonascia, J., & Meinert, C. L. (1997). Results at age 8 years of early intervention for low-birthweight premature infants. *Journal of the American Medical Association, 277,* 126–132.

McCormick, M. C. (1989). Long-term follow-up of infants discharged from neonatal intensive care units. *Journal of the American Medical Association, 261,* 1767–1772.

McLoyd, V. C. (1990). The impact of economic hardship on black families and children: Psychological distress, parenting, and socioemotional status. *Child Development, 61,* 311–346.

Mellins, C. A., Levenson, R. L., Zawadzki, R., Kairam, R., & Weston, M. (1994). Effects of pediatric HIV infection and prenatal drug exposure on mental and psychomotor development. *Journal of Pediatric Psychology, 19,* 617–627.

Messinger, D., Dolcourt, J., King, J., Bodnar, A., & Beck, D. (1996). The survival and developmental outcome of extremely low birth weight infants. *Infant Mental Health Journal, 17,* 375–385.

Milani-Comparetti, A., & Gidoni, E. A. (1967). Routine developmental examination in normal and retarded children. *Developmental Medicine and Child Neurology, 9,* 631–636.

National Commission on Children. (1991). *Beyond rhetoric: A new American agenda for children and families.* Washington, DC: Author.

Nellis, L., & Gridley, B. E. (1994). Review of the Bayley Scales of Infant Development–Second edition. *Journal of School Psychology, 32,* 201–209.

Newborg, J., Stock, J. R., Wnek, L., Guidubaldi, J., & Svinicki, J. (1984). *The Battelle Developmental Inventory.* Allen, TX: DLM Teaching Resources.

Oates, R. R., Peacock, A., & Forrest, D. (1984). Long-term effects of nonorganic failure to thrive. *Pediatrics, 75,* 36–40.

Phatak, P. (1993). Baroda Norms of Motor and Mental Development of Indian babies from 1 to 30 months. *Psychological Studies, 38,* 142–149.

Preyer, W. (1882). *Die Seele des Kindes.* Leipzig: Fernan. In *The mind of the child* (1888–1889) vol. 1, 2. New York: Appleton.

Ramey, C. T., & Campbell, F. A. (1991). Poverty, early childhood education, and academic competence: The Abecedarian experiment. In A. C. Huston (Ed.), *Children in poverty: Child development and public policy* (pp. 190–221). Cambridge, MA: Cambridge University Press.

Robinson, B. F., & Mervis, C. B. (1996). Extrapolated raw scores for the second edition of the Bayley Scales of Infant Development. *American Journal on Mental Retardation, 100,* 666–670.

Rose, S. A., & Feldman, J. F. (1995). Prediction of IQ and specific cognitive abilities at 11 years from infancy measures. *Developmental Psychology, 31,* 685–696.

Ross, G., & Lawson, K. (1997). Using the Bayley-II: Unresolved issues in assessing the development of prematurely born children. *Journal of Developmental and Behavioral Pediatrics, 18,* 109–111.

Rossman, M. J., Hyman, S. L., Rorabaugh, M. L., Berlin, L. E., Allen, M. C., & Modlin, J. F. (1994). The CAT/CLAMS assessment for early intervention services. Clinical Adaptive Test/Clinical Linguistic and Auditory Milestone Scale. *Clinical Pediatrics, 33,* 404–409.

Ruff, H. A., & Rothbart M. K. (1996). *Attention in early development.* New York: Oxford University Press.

Russell, D., Palisano, R., Walter, S., Rosenbaum, P., Gemus, M., Gowland, C., Galuppi, B., & Lane, M. (1998). Evaluating motor function in children with Down syndrome: Validity of the GMFM. *Developmental Medicine and Child Neurology, 40,* 693–701.

Sajaniemi, N., Salokorpi, T., & von Wendt, L. (1998). Temperament profiles and their role in neurodevelopmental assessed preterm children at two years of age. *European Child and Adolescent Psychiatry, 7,* 145–152.

Sameroff, A. J., & Chandler, M. J. (1975). Reproductive risk and the continuum of caretaking casualty. In F. D. Horowitz (Ed.), *Review of child development research.* (Vol. 4, pp. 187–244). Chicago: University of Chicago Press.

Sattler, J. M. (1992). *Assessment of Children.* (3rd ed.). San Diego: Author.

Schweinhart, L. J., & Weikart, D. P. (1989). The High/Scope Perry preschool study: Implications for early childhood care and education. *Prevention in Human Services, 7,* 109–132.

Sears, R. R., Maccoby, E. E., & Levin, H. (1957). *Patterns of child rearing.* Evanston, IL: Row, Peterson.

Shen, X. M., Yan, C. H., Guo, D., Wu, S. M., Li, R. Q., Huang, H., Ao, L. M., Zhou, J. D., Hong, Z. Y., Xu, J. D., Jin, X. M., & Tang, J. M. (1998). Low-level prenatal lead exposure and neurobehavioral development of children in the first year of life: A prospective study in Shanghai. *Environmental Research, 79,* 1–8.

Shonkoff, J. P., Hauser-Cram, P., Krauss, M. W., & Upshur, C. C. (1992). Development of infants with disabilities and their families. *Monographs of the Society for Research in Child Development, 57*(6) [230] v–153.

Siegel, L. S. (1981). Infant tests as predictors of cognitive and language development at 2 years. *Child Development, 52,* 545–537.

Siegel, L. S. (1982). Early cognitive and environmental correlates of language development at 4 years. *International Journal of Behavioral Development, 5,* 433–444.

Siegel, L. S., Cooper, D. C., Fitzhardinge, P. M., & Ash, A. J. (1995). The use of the Mental Development Index of the Bayley Scale to diagnose language delay in 2-year-old high risk infants. *Infant Behavior and Development, 18,* 483–486.

Sigman, M., Neumann, C., Carter, E., & Cattle, D. J., D'Souza, S., & Bwibo, N. (1988). Home interactions and the development of Embu toddlers in Kenya. *Child Development, 59,* 1251–1261.

Sparrow, S. S., Bulla, D. A., & Cicchetti, D. V. (1984). *Vineland Adaptive Behavior Scales.* Circle Pines, MN: American Guidance Service.

Spreen, O., Risser, A. H., & Edgell, D. (1995). *Developmental neuropsychology.* New York: Oxford University Press.

Tasbihsazan, R., Nettelbeck, T., & Kirby, N. (1997). Increasing Mental Development Index in Australian children: A comparative study of two versions of the Bayley Mental Scale. *Australian Psychologist, 32,* 120–125.

Thompson, B., Wasserman, J. D., & Matula, K. (1996). The factor structure of the Behavior Rating Scale of the Bayley Scales of Infant Development–II. *Educational and Psychological Measurement, 56,* 460–474.

Uzgiris, I. C., & Hunt, J. M. (1975). *Assessment in infancy: Ordinal scales of psychological development.* Urbana: University of Illinois Press.

Washington, K., Scott, D. T., Johnson, K. A., Wendel, S., & Hay, A. E. (1998). The Bayley Scales of Infant Development–II and children with developmental delays: A clinical perspective. *Journal of Developmental and Behavioral Pediatrics, 19,* 346–349.

Werner, E. E., Bierman, J. M., & French, F. E. (1971). *The children of Kauai: A longitudinal study from the prenatal period to age 10.* Honolulu: University of Hawaii Press.

Werner, E. E., & Smith, R. S. (1982). *Vulnerable but invisible: A longitudinal study of resilient children and youth.* New York: McGraw & Hill.

Wolf, A. W., & Lozoff, B. (1985). A clinically interpretable method for analyzing the Bayley Infant Behavior Record. *Journal of Pediatric Psychology, 10,* 199–214.

Zimmerman, I. L., Steiner, V. G., & Pond, R. E. (1992). *Preschool Language Scale–3.* San Antonio, TX: Psychological Corporation.

Annotated Bibliography

Aylward, G. P. (1994). *Practitioner's guide to developmental and psychological testing.* New York: Plenum.

This book provides a comprehensive review of developmental and psychological tests (including the BSID-II) that are commonly used to evaluate children who are suspected of being developmentally delayed or have difficulties in school performance. It is written for clinicians and provides an overview of tests, including their strength and limitations, and applications to clinical practice.

Aylward, G. P. (1997). *Infant and early childhood neuropsychology.* New York: Plenum Press.

This book examines the brain-behavior changes that occur during infancy in the emerging interdisciplinary field of infant and early childhood neuropsychology. It provides an excellent background in both normal and abnormal development that enables infant examiners to have a better understanding of the developmental processes measured by the BSID-II.

Bayley, N. (1993). *Manual for the Bayley Scales of Infant Development* (2nd ed.). San Antonio, TX: Psychological Corporation.

The manual is included in the BSID-II kit. It provides specific information on how to administer, score, and interpret the items in the BSID-II, along with norms tables for the Mental, Motor, and Behavior Rating Scales. In addition, it includes background information on the development and standardization of the BSID-II, including data on validity and reliability. Four case studies are included that illustrate how the BSID-II can be used in clinical practice.

Bremmer, G., Slater, A., & Butterworth, G. (Eds.). *Infant development: Recent advances.* Hove, England: Psychology Press/Erlbaum (UK) Taylor & Francis.

This edited volume addresses recent research and theoretical developments in infant development. It presents similarities and contrasts regarding theories of early development, with chapters organized into sections on perceptual, cognitive, and social development. New findings on infant perception and dynamic systems theory are included. This review provides a theoretical basis in normal development that is useful for infant examiners.

Goldstein, D. J., Fogle, E. E., Wieber, J. L., & O'Shea, T. M. (1995). Comparison of the Bayley Scales of Infant Development–Second Edition and the Bayley Scales of Infant Development with premature infants. *Journal of Psychoeducational Assessment, 13,* 391–396.

This article compares the scores of premature infants tested on the BSID and BSID-II. It provides information on the psychometric properties of the two scales that could be useful to examiners who use both scales.

Hanson, M. J. (1996). *Atypical infant development.* Austin, TX: Pro-Ed, Inc.

This book examines comprehensive care for infants born disabled or at risk for subsequent developmental delay. It uses a multidisciplinary perspective to emphasize the importance of early intervention and family support.

Mercer, J. (1998). *Infant development: A multidisciplinary perspective.* Pacific Grove, CA: Brooks/Cole Publishing Co.

This is a basic text that examines the complexities of infant development, including cultural and gender issues. It is written in a useful style that includes vocabulary terms, problems to consider and discuss, a description of "the integrated baby" that emphasizes how infant systems work together, boxed sections titled "Applications & Arguments."

Robinson, B. F., & Mervis, C. B. (1996). Extrapolated raw scores for the second edition of the Bayley Scales of Infant Development. *American Journal on Mental Retardation, 100,* 666–670.

This article includes extrapolated raw scores for the BSID-II for infants with estimated index scores between 30 and 50. Examiners should remember that these scores are not based on empirical data. Extrapolated scoring should be used with caution and with full disclosure. However, extrapolated scoring enables examiners to describe children's performance in more detail than reporting an index score <50.

Ross, G., & Lawson, K. (1997). Using the Bayley-II: Unresolved issues in assessing the development of prematurely born children. *Journal of Developmental and Behavioral Pediatrics, 18,* 109–111.

This article examines the use of item sets among infants born prematurely. It raises concerns about the choice of item sets and when age correction should be applied among premature infants.

Washington, K., Scott, D. T., Johnson, K. A., Wendel, S., & Hay, A. E. (1998). The Bayley Scales of Infant Development–II and children with developmental delays: A clinical perspective. *Journal of Developmental and Behavioral Pediatrics, 19,* 346–349.

The authors discuss concerns about the use of item sets when evaluating children who have developmental delays. They present several case studies illustrating how choice of item sets can vary results. Examiners should be aware of these concerns in making their choice regarding item sets.

Index